MW01002991

HOW TO MAKE
COMMUNITY
YOUR **COMPETITIVE**
ADVANTAGE

THE
BUSINESS
OF
BELONGING

DAVID
SPINKS

WILEY

Published by John Wiley & Sons, Inc., Hoboken, New Jersey.

Published simultaneously in Canada.

For general information on our other products and services or for technical support, please contact our Customer Care Department within the United States at (800) 762-2974, outside the United States at (317) 572-3993 or fax (317) 572-4002.

Wiley publishes in a variety of print and electronic formats and by print-on-demand. Some material included with standard print versions of this book may not be included in e-books or in print-on-demand. If this book refers to media such as a CD or DVD that is not included in the version you purchased, you may download this material at http://booksupport.wiley.com. For more information about Wiley products, visit www.wiley.com.

Library of Congress Cataloging-in-Publication Data

Names: Spinks, David, author.
Title: The business of belonging : how to make community your competitive advantage / by David Spinks.
Description: Hoboken, New Jersey : Wiley, [2021] | Includes bibliographical references and index.
Identifiers: LCCN 2020053682 (print) | LCCN 2020053683 (ebook) | ISBN 9781119766124 (cloth) | ISBN 9781119766148 (adobe pdf) | ISBN 9781119766117 (epub)
Subjects: LCSH: Customer relations.
Classification: LCC HF5415.5 .S68 2021 (print) | LCC HF5415.5 (ebook) | DDC 658.8/12–dc23
LC record available at https://lccn.loc.gov/2020053682
LC ebook record available at https://lccn.loc.gov/2020053683

Cover Design: Paul McCarthy
Cover Image: © Getty Images | Lushik

SKY10027806_062421

For Alison

Contents

Foreword

In 2016, I agreed to speak at the CMX Summit in the Palace of Fine Arts in San Francisco. It was still a relatively new conference, just a couple years old, and it proclaimed to focus entirely on community management. As a longtime community founder, I didn't know what to expect. At every other startup or marketing conference I had been to (and I had been to a lot), community building was usually a footnote on the agenda. But from the moment I arrived, I knew this event was different. Everywhere I turned seemed to be conversations, people, and products focused on building community. To my shock, as I sat in a dense crowd of hundreds of people, I felt something I hadn't felt since I started building my community six years before: true professional belonging.

The conference was started by David Spinks. We had first met a few weeks before the conference and I immediately recognized that he cared about and deeply understood what I cared about: building communities. But the way he spoke about community and how it would change the world of business wasn't something I heard anyone talking about at that time. He was sure that in the near future, every business would be building community. And he was dedicating his life to that cause.

My own journey of building a community-driven business dates back to 2010 when a few friends and I began hosting events called Startup Grind in my small office in Mountain View, California. At first it didn't seem like much of anything special—just a couple dozen startup people meeting up and networking. But the momentum soon started to build. Ten people at the first event turned into 20, then 50, then 100, then 250.

At one event, an attendee approached me and asked me if he could launch a Startup Grind chapter in Los Angeles. The culture we had built at Startup Grind around the values of giving first, helping others, and making friends were actually very unique in the startup world at the time. They wanted to bring that mentality to LA. And it worked! Soon, the LA chapter was growing quickly.

After the success in LA, we started inviting our members to kick off their own local chapters in their city. Today, Startup Grind has 600 active chapters in 120 countries. We've hosted 15,000 events led by 2,000 volunteers. Most of what we did was self-taught, fumbling around in the dark until we figured out enough wrong ways to build our community to find the right things to do.

As a battle-scarred community builder, discovering CMX and meeting David that day in 2016 was like returning home after being gone on a long, impossible journey. At CMX, for the first time I was in a place where other people were speaking my community language. Each attendee seemed to be engaged in their own epic community building journey. I found myself nodding at every speaker's insights and having to hold back on all my questions.

When people ask me to describe David Spinks, I affectionately tell them that he is the Yoda or Dalai Lama of community (much to his chagrin). This isn't just because David is one of the most genuine and thoughtful people I have met, but because he is the first person I met that put frameworks and science behind the things that I had been building. The SPACES model was the first true business case for building a community. The language and tools he put forth in the industry have become staples in the process of building branded communities today.

Over the last ten years, David's advice has been sought by the very best companies in the world to help them figure out how to craft and grow an authentic community with their customers. Leaders from the top communities come to CMX to dispense their knowledge to the rest of the industry.

Tens of thousands of decision makers have already benefited from David's experiences and frameworks, but probably no one more than me. In a veiled excuse to spend more time working near him, in early 2019, my company Bevy acquired CMX so that we could be part of the community revolution that he helped pioneer.

Having worked side by side with him since then, I have been thrilled to see the *Business of Belonging* finally come to light as our company has grown 10X since David joined, in large part due to implementing many of the principles that he shares in this book. I truly believe that this book will become the bible that every community builder reads.

When competitors' product features and functionality are the same as yours, having a community is, as David eloquently says, "The one thing they can't copy." At a time when no one wants to click on another digital ad, your community can fire up your sales channel or turn a detractor into a promoter. If I had this book when I started Startup Grind, I can only imagine how much further I would be and how many mistakes I could have avoided.

As you study and apply the lessons in this book, hopefully you will feel what I felt at that first CMX event I attended: a connection to the people who have trodden the path you're on or embarking on, and that there is a fountain of support and lessons you can benefit from to help you on your own community building journey.

Derek Andersen
Co-Founder, Startup Grind, Bevy

Introduction

The internet was where I first found a sense of belonging. It was back in middle school. I was a kid growing up in the suburbs of New York City, and didn't fit in.

Both of my parents were immigrants. My dad was born in Ireland, moved to Israel where he met my mother, got married, moved to the US, and I was born one year later. We didn't have a deeply rooted social network in our local community. We were new, and different. We had some extended family nearby, but most of our family lived in other countries. I was a bit awkward and tried too hard to fit in. I was bullied for being Jewish and having a parent with an accent. As I grew up, I found myself disconnected from early childhood friends, and I struggled mightily to find my social rhythm.

Despite not fitting in, I was still someone who felt *strongly* drawn to other people. I loved organizing and being a part of social activities. I loved meeting new people. For better or worse, I needed people to like and engage with me in order for me to like myself. And I would get deeply depressed when I was turned away by the groups I cared most about.

When I couldn't find community locally, I was forced to search elsewhere. I ended up finding it in online video games. *Tony Hawk's Pro Skater 4* was one of the first console games developed specifically to be played online. I picked it up and quickly became addicted. In truth, I think I was more addicted to the social network on the game than the game itself.

I became one of the top competitive THPS4 players in the world and had developed a strong reputation on the game. I decided with a couple friends to start up a clan and we quickly rose to the top of the clan rankings. We launched a website and a forum, which became one of the most popular online communities for THPS4 players at the time.

We had a really tight-knit community with lots of shared stories and inside jokes. I once won a personal meet-and-greet with Mr. Hawk himself and asked him if he could sign a Jell-O pudding pack for me. It was an inside joke in our community, and we planned to give it away in a contest. He looked very confused when I handed it to him but just kind of smirked and signed it anyway. Probably not the best idea to get a valuable autograph on a perishable good, but it was totally worth it for the reaction from the community.

I was just 14, still in middle school, and would sprint home every day to get online, play games, and manage a community with hundreds of active members. We hosted competitions, created video content, dealt with trolls and spam, launched and relaunched forums, empowered moderators from the community … all the things that anyone who manages an online community does today. I had not only found belonging, but I was creating community and belonging for others. It was the greatest feeling in the world! From that point on, I was hooked on community building. I became obsessed with how the internet could be a platform for community and started engaging in every online community I could find. I joined more gaming communities, started sharing poetry and journaling online and became an early adopter of every new social platform.

It was at college that I started connecting community to the world of business.

I was a business administration major. The problem was, all of the courses in the program felt super outdated. We were being taught things that worked for businesses 10 years ago. Meanwhile, I was witnessing a social revolution taking place on the internet. Blogging was wildly popular at the time. Every college student in the US was using Facebook every day. A strange social platform called Twitter was starting to grow in popularity. It seemed obvious to me that business would all be driven by online communities and social spaces. But none of my classes even mentioned the internet.

So I pitched the business department on launching a course focused on online communities. They said no. Womp womp. Luckily, my computer science teacher was more receptive and said if I helped create the curriculum, he would make it a course in his department. The next semester we kicked off the school's first online community and social media course. I soon had the opportunity to start doing paid community building work, organizing community events, and programming for the college union. I also launched our school's first-ever official blog, which is still going today.

Becoming a Community Professional

While in college, I started a personal blog to write about what I was learning in the world of community, social internet, and business, and started making a name for myself. The founders of a startup called Scribnia, Russell D'Souza and Jack Groetzinger, read one of my blog posts and emailed me asking me to be their first *community manager.* Just like that, I had my first official job building community for a business!

It turned out that building community for a business was a lot different from building a community for a video game or for college students. Customer communities were a totally different beast. Members' motivations were different, expectations were higher, I had to have goals and metrics and report on my success … I had to become a community "professional."

> "No problem!," I thought. "I'll just find mentors and training programs to teach me how to build community on a professional level!"

Well … it turned out there really weren't many people with experience building communities for companies back then. People didn't understand what it meant to build community for a business. They were still thinking about it like traditional marketing, using social platforms to build an audience rather than connect people to each other.

It truly was a brand new profession. I realized I was largely on my own.

Slowly, I started meeting other people who, like me, were building real communities for businesses. I ended up starting a blog and job board called TheCommunityManager.com with my friends Jenn Pedde and Brett Petersel who were also community managers. We started publishing regular articles about what we were learning, and invited other community professionals to do the same. We organized meetups, and just started creating spaces for people who did this kind of work to connect and support each other.

My role as the director of community for a startup called Zaarly and started a couple companies of my own, including a somewhat spontaneous two-year swing at building an online cooking school called Feast with my roommate Nadia Eghbal. After giving it a good go, we were running out of investor money and losing interest; it was looking like Feast was going to be a bust. Nadia would go on to become a principal at Collaborative Fund and work on community at GitHub and Substack. And I had a new opportunity fall into my lap that would define the rest of my career.

Building the Community Industry

As fate would have it, my friend and fellow entrepreneur Max Altschuler came to me with a proposition at the perfect time. I had told him in the past that I had a dream of hosting a conference entirely focused on the community industry. He wanted to help me start it.

This was five years after I got my first community manager job, and more businesses were starting to invest in community. I was meeting hundreds of community professionals, some of whom were doing incredible work for well-known brands. But their work was still going unnoticed in the broader business community. I felt that if we could organize a legitimate conference for community professionals, it would bring more credibility and awareness to the community industry, help community professionals level up their work, and motivate more companies to invest in community.

Max said he would handle all the logistics for the event since he had experience running a conference, and I could focus on curating speakers and marketing. I figured why not, I have anything to lose, and CMX Summit was born.

Launching CMX felt like the culmination of everything I learned and worked on in my life and career. That first event was one of the most powerful community experiences I ever felt. We had 300 people come from around the world. It was the first conference where every single person in the room was building community for a business.

Attendees didn't know what to expect. They were so used to being the only community professional at an event, and having to explain what they do a hundred times because no one understood what community management actually was.

We took a very different tone at the event than what community professionals were used to. The title "community manager" was perceived as low value, junior level, nice-to-have. It wasn't well defined or respected.

At CMX, we told them that that community would be the future of business, and that they're doing the most important work in the world.

We put speakers on stage who successfully built community programs up at companies like Lyft, Airbnb, 500 Startups, and Apple. We told them community is extremely valuable, their profession is important, and we're at the start of something huge.

One attendee from that very first conference, Holly Firestone, who was running community for Atlassian at the time and would go on to lead community teams for Salesforce, wrote many years later about the impact CMX Summit had on her career.

> I remember pulling up to the event, and I was so excited. I felt like a kid on her first day of school. I remember what I was wearing. White shirt, green jacket, jeans, brown boots, and a bright blue scarf. I remember exactly how the room looked. It was crowded with people in every inch of the space. I just looked around in awe. I couldn't believe that everyone in the room was there for a community management conference [...] When I think about what was most valuable to me that day, it was that I was surrounded by people with which I didn't need to push back. A huge weight that I had been carrying around was lifted off of me. I finally felt, without a doubt, I was making the right decision about my career. I left feeling inspired and reinvigorated. This was a huge turning point for me.

It was the sentiment that we heard from a lot of the attendees that day. It was the first time they were surrounded by people who understood what it meant to be a community professional. It was the first time they felt like there was a real career path for them in the world of business. It was a space where, for the first time, they didn't feel alone in their work.

I knew that there was something special happening here and felt like I found the work I was meant to do. I turned my full-time focus to building CMX. We made it our mission to advance the community industry and help community professionals thrive. I wanted community professionals to have all the resources I wish I had when I first kicked off my career in community.

The Community Era Has Arrived

Fast forward, and the CMX community has grown to tens of thousands of members, we've hosted numerous global conferences and have over 60 local, volunteer-led chapters around the world. I get to do what I love every day: build, research, and teach community. After five years of bootstrapping, CMX was acquired by the community and virtual events software platform Bevy, which helped both of us accelerate our growth and impact. I've had the opportunity to work with teams at companies like Google, Airbnb, National Geographic, Redbull, Facebook, Waze, Udemy, Salesforce, Atlassian, and hundreds more through workshops and consulting. And I've learned a lot about what it takes to launch, manage, and scale successful community programs that create genuine belonging for members and measurable value for businesses.

Our prediction at that first CMX Summit that community was the future of business has proven true. A recent study by First Round Capital found that 80 percent of startups today are already investing in community and 28 percent consider it to be their "moat and critical to their success."[1] In our own study of companies investing in community, 88 percent said that community is critical to their company's mission.[2] It's hard to find a company today that isn't at least thinking about community.

Even with the increased attention, there's still a lot of uncertainty around how to invest in community. There isn't a human out there that would argue that community isn't important. The question isn't whether or not community is important. For a business that has to optimize every dollar spent and ruthlessly prioritize what it focuses on, the question is, "Why should we invest in community over all of the other things we could be investing in?" And once you're ready to make that investment, how does a business build a legitimate community that creates authentic belonging for members, while also driving business outcomes? Can you measure it? How do you know it's working? What does a successful community look like?

These are the questions I've spent my whole career working to answer. And these days, a week doesn't go by that I'm not asked by a number of businesses who are trying to figure it out.

I wrote this book to provide you with the answers. I've been writing this book for three years, but gathering the lessons and insights for this book for more than 10 years. It's a collection of everything I've learned and studied in the world of community-driven business.

After reading this book, I want you to understand what it means to be a community-driven business. I want you to understand how to drive higher trust, lower costs, and scale every part of the customer and sales journey in a way traditional businesses can only dream. I want you to have everything you need to build real belonging for your people and make community your competitive advantage.

Let's do this.

Notes

1. "First Round State of Startups 2019," stateofstartups2019.firstround.com, 2019, https://stateofstartups2019.fifoorstround.com/.
2. "2020 Community Industry Trends Report," *CMX* (CMX, 2019), https://cmxhub.com/community-industry-trends-report-2020.

Chapter 1

Why Community Is the New Competitive Advantage

What does it actually mean for a business to build community? It's such a broad term that's used in so many different ways, it's always difficult to nail down. In every conversation I have with a company asking for advice on their community strategy, I always kick off by asking, "Why are you investing in community?" The majority of the time, this is the first time anyone at the company has had to articulate an answer to that question.

So we're going to start there. In this chapter, I'm going to give you some working definitions of community, we'll talk about the history of businesses investing in community, and I'll help you understand why it's becoming such a prominent part of the conversation today. I'll also share some big-picture concepts that explain why community is such a powerful force for businesses. We're starting high-level, and will get more and more specific as we move through the book.

Let's start off with some history ...

A Customer Community Is Born

Business has been moving in the direction of community for a long time now. In fact, if you go looking for the very first time a business built a community team, you'd have to go back to the early days of the internet.

Apple pioneered a new wave of computing. But did you know it was also the very first company to have a community team and build a customer community program?

1

There weren't many places for people to talk to each other online when Ellen Petry Leanse joined the company in 1981 as a communications specialist, just five years after the company was founded. In 1985, after the Mac launched, Apple was dealing with frustration at the hands of its users – especially those who had committed to the Apple II in the years before the Mac. As the company pivoted toward the Mac in 1984, they felt abandoned, and most of the feedback received from customers came in the form of printed letters mailed to their office.

Leanse would respond to these letters directly and started noticing that a lot of the letters had a code on them. When she asked the customers about the codes, she learned that they were access codes for BBS groups (bulletin board systems). Unbeknownst to Apple, their customers were already gathering online on one of the earliest forms of internet forums, and talking about their products.

Leanse saw an opportunity. She advocated – against resistance, since "going online" was uncharted territory for any tech enterprise at that time – for establishing their own BBS node and sharing information from Apple directly with its user communities. Suddenly they were connected with a global community of customers.

It was an uphill battle for Leanse. If you think engaging in online communities is unfamiliar territory for businesses today, you can imagine what it felt like back then. Participating in communities with customers just wasn't something businesses did. Even Apple, who's well known for breaking the mold, was hesitant, largely viewing users as a "cost," not a benefit.

Ellen fought for making a real investment in community. She would spend a lot of time talking to customers, gathering their feedback, and sharing it internally. After a lot of advocacy, she found a believer in Apple's CEO, John Sculley, who backed taking the voice of users seriously. With his support, the "Apple User Group Connection" was born, led by Leanse. "I was fortunate enough to be chosen to make this connection, and I couldn't have done it alone – but I did fight for it alone", said Leanse. "no one knew anything about it until after I started sharing with users and harnessing the power of their input."

The AUGC was a hit, bringing together Apple users from around the world and providing a channel for their voice to be heard. Sculley would host digital discussions in the user groups, sharing updates with users and listening to their feedback. It opened up the curtains in a way businesses just didn't do at that time, and it helped Apple turn the corner on improving customer sentiment.

"We felt it start to humanize the company at a time when technology was all about the machine," says Leanse.

It was a revolutionary mentality for a business to adopt at the time, and a preview of what was to come.

The Rise of Community-Driven Business

Apple was early to identify an important trend that would accelerate over the next few decades: the growing power of the customer.

Back when customers couldn't talk to each other or research products (unless they were more technical and could use tools like BBS groups), companies didn't have to prioritize customer support. If customers had a bad experience, they wouldn't be able to tell too many other people about it.

That all changed when customers could suddenly talk to each other online using social networks. They could now share reviews of products, "word of mouth" was accelerated, and positive or negative sentiment could spread like wildfire.

This led to the huge customer service trend, led by companies like Zappos and Amazon. In his book *Delivering Happiness,* Zappos CEO Tony Hsieh recalled the radical perspective they had on growing the business. "Our philosophy [was] to take most of the money we would have spent on paid advertising and invest it into customer service and the customer experience instead, letting our customers do the marketing for us through word of mouth."[1]

This was unheard of at the time, and it worked! Zappos would grow to be the internet's largest shoe retailer, and it sparked a revolution in how businesses would look at customers. Putting the customer first became a competitive advantage.

This trend grew as social networks continued to give consumers more power and access. Companies started hiring full content and social media teams to build trust and to connect more personally with customers. "Inbound marketing" and "customer success" was born to proactively invest in helping customers succeed. Businesses started making it a priority to help customers more successfully use their products, improve their skills, and grow in their careers, knowing that a more successful customer is a more loyal customer.

But it was still very much one-to-one and "one-to-many" communication. It would be a company rep talking to a customer directly, or creating content that would be distributed to a large audience. What most companies were failing to do, save for a few exceptions like Apple, was create spaces for "many-to-many" communication. With one-to-one, you're limited by how many people you can form deep trust and connection with. With one-to-many communication, you can reach more people, but will lack depth. With many-to-many communication, there is no limit.

That's why we're now seeing customer support and content marketing give way to a new era of customer relationships: the customer community.

This next phase is all about helping customers and other stakeholders connect to each other. Companies are setting themselves apart by tapping into the collective energy, knowledge, and contributions of your most passionate customers, fans, and partners. When people feel like they're a part of a community it becomes their home. They don't want to leave. And they'll step up to contribute and grow the community in ways you can't imagine.

There are few better examples of companies who have tapped into the power of community than Salesforce. Erica Kuhl spent the majority of her 17 years at Salesforce building the community program from the ground up. Kuhl once described herself to me as a "bulldog" who would not give up on something she believed in. She certainly didn't when it came to community. Much like Ellen Leanse at Apple, the company didn't "get it," and she fought a long, uphill battle to get leadership to understand what it meant to build community and why it was such a big opportunity. Lucky for Salesforce, they trusted her and gave her a chance to prove it.

She knew that the only true way to get buy-in was with data, and she made it a priority to show how community could impact the bottom line. Whenever she took on a new community project, she made sure it would be something she could measure, and tie back to ROI.

Over the years she was able to show how community reduced support costs, increased product adoption, and increased customer spend and retention. She would become Salesforce's first VP of Community and community would get woven into the fabric of every product at Salesforce. There are now over 3,000,000 members in the Salesforce Trailblazer community supporting and educating each other in how to better use the product and grow in their careers. Recent research conducted by the company showed that 82 percent of its customers found that the community increased the ROI of their investment in Salesforce's tools, and 93 percent said that it helped them find new products and tools they could use in the Salesforce product suite.

Every day, we're seeing more examples of companies driving incredible results by building community. One recent study showed that over half of the Fortune Global 50 and the 50 highest-valued startups in the world are investing in community programs.[2]

Newer companies that have risen in the community-driven business era have made community a priority from day one, and prioritized building community before they even started building a product. Take collaborative design tool Figma as an example. Figma was originally built as a community for designers to meet and communicate. The founders believed that design should be collaborative and live online, so they started building a software product for their community to use. Today over a million designers use Figma, and they're valued at $2 billion after just 8 years in business. The knowledge-base app Notion is another great example of a company that has focused on community from day one, creating collaborative platforms for users to share their templates with each other and forming a cult following. Or look at the notes tool Roam Research whose customers literally refer to themselves as the "Roam Cult" and you can see community woven into the fabric of everything they do.

We're also seeing the rise of community entrepreneurship, where the community is the product. For many years, large social platforms like Facebook and Reddit had a monopoly on online communities. But we're seeing an explosion of independent community businesses like Indie Hackers, the community for bootstrapping entrepreneurs that was acquired by Stripe; Product Hunt, the community for sharing and discovering new products that was acquired by Angel List;

and Her, the community for LGBTQ+ womxn with over 4 million users. These "community-first" businesses are growing fast, and they provide a model for financially sustainable communities.

The number of companies that make building community a priority is only going to keep growing.

Giving Customers a True Sense of Community

Before we go much deeper into the business value, it's important to understand what I mean when I use the term *community*.

Community is a *really* broad term. If you ask a hundred people "What is a community?" you'll get a hundred different answers.

It's a shared identity! It's shared passion! It's people who care about each other! It's a neighborhood! It's religion! It's a belief! It's family! It's a fanbase! It's my friends! It's a sports team!

The range of definitions of community can literally range from all of the people in the world, to just a few, depending on the context. Social scientists and community experts have spent decades working to articulate exactly what makes a group of people a "community."

The one theory that has always resonated most with me, and the one that has been most influential on recent research in the field of community psychology, is called the *sense of community theory*, created by social psychologists David McMillan and David Chavis in 1986.[3]

The authors describe a sense of community as "a feeling that members have of belonging, a feeling that members matter to one another and to the group, and a shared faith that members' needs will be met through their commitment to be together."

According to the theory, there are four factors that contribute to a sense of community: membership, influence, integration/fulfillment of needs, and shared emotional connection.

Membership

Membership is the feeling of belonging or of sharing a sense of personal relatedness and includes five attributes:

1. *Boundaries*. How do people become members, and what are the boundaries keeping others out?

2. *Emotional safety.* By building boundaries and including the right people, you create trust and a feeling of safety.
3. *A sense of belonging and identification.* Members must feel like they fit in and that this is "their community."
4. *Personal investment.* If members contribute or make sacrifices to the community, it enhances their sense of community.
5. *A common symbol system.* Sharing a symbol like a sports team jersey or a brand logo creates a sense of community.

Influence

The second element is influence, or a sense of mattering. It has to work both ways, with members feeling like they have influence over the community and the community having influence over the members.

Influence also speaks to the concept of giving first before asking for anything. The theory states that:

> People who acknowledge that others' needs, values, and opinions matter to them are often the most influential group members, while those who always push to influence, try to dominate others, and ignore the wishes and opinions of others are often the least powerful members.

So it's important to create an environment in your community where members feel like they have a say in what happens. Each member should know that someone is listening, no matter what, even if it's just the community manager.

And for a community to have influence over its members, it simply has to become a place that they care about. It has to provide them with value that they don't want to lose.

Integration and Fulfillment of Needs

This essentially means that by joining a community, members get what they hoped to get by joining.

It reinforces the idea that your community, like any other product, needs to solve a problem for its members in order to make it worth their time and contribution.

A reward might be something specific like an answer to a question or networking. Or it could be something a bit more intangible, like a sense of belonging, a feeling of purpose, a new friend, etc. Members need to feel rewarded in some way for their participation in the community in order to continue to contribute.

This is why it's important to talk to your users and get a good idea of who they are. Then you can understand their needs and how the community can best serve them.

Shared Emotional Connection

All healthy communities have a story. Members will have a history of experiences together and the belief that there will be more experiences together in the future.

These experiences form a long-lasting, emotion connection. That's why a community that goes through a crisis often comes out much stronger because they've now shared a difficult situation, forging a strong emotional bond amongst members.

This factor is believed to be the "definitive element for true community" by the authors.

You can use these four factors to better understand the strength of community that a group has. All groups of people have the potential to be a strong community. But without clearly defined membership, an exchange of influence, fulfillment of needs, and a shared emotional connection, it's fair to assume that the strength of community amongst a group is pretty weak.

There are lots of companies that throw around the term *community,* using it to describe their customers and audience regardless of whether or not there's an actual deep sense of community amongst the people they're referring to.

I urge you to think about how to create real community for your people, rather than just slapping the title onto everything. Because if you can create a true sense of community for people, that's what will make them care enough to contribute. And that's what will unlock all the business value we'll talk about in this book.

The Unrivaled Scalability of Community

When you give people a true sense of community, it motivates them to want to get involved and contribute. Motivate enough people, and community can help you achieve incredible scale.

One company that's succeeded at scaling by creating a true community for many of its members is Duolingo, led by their incredible Global Head of Community, Laura Nestler. The language learning app does everything with a community-first mindset and it's enabled them to achieve incredible scale in a relatively short time, having launched publicly in 2012 and offering nearly 100 different courses to their userbase of over 300 million.

Developing 100 language learning courses takes an incredible amount of resources. Contrast Duolingo with the language-learning software Rosetta Stone, which was founded in 1992 and only offers 23 languages. Duolingo did this all with just over 300 employees. Rosetta Stone has over 1,300 employees. Today, Duolingo is (privately) valued at over $1.5 billion, and Rosetta Stone's market cap is about $700 million.

The secret to Duolingo's scale? You guessed it … community! The majority of courses on Duolingo are developed with the help of the community. Duolingo's learning scientists and curriculum experts provide structure and guidance, as well as review all content before it goes live. However, the community contributes the content and translations that make the actual courses.

The product isn't the only thing powered by community at Duolingo. When they found that their users wanted to practice languages with each other in-person, Duolingo took a community-first approach. They asked their most motivated members if they'd be interested in organizing local events where learners could come and practice their language with each other. Today, a team of three people at Duolingo is responsible for running over 2,600 events per month.

It's the kind of scale that companies dream of. And it can only be achieved by taking a community approach. By giving your customers the opportunity to connect with and support each other, you can deliver exponentially more value at a fraction of the cost of traditional business tactics.

That doesn't mean you should hire a junior community manager and expect them to run 1,000 events. You need to invest properly into the right people and systems in order to set community up to succeed. With the right foundation in place, the sky is the limit for how much they can accomplish.

When talking about the value of community, people often focus on customer retention, and how being a part of a community will make customers more loyal. This value is big and shouldn't be ignored, but the BIG competitive advantage comes from how you activate those loyal customers to contribute their energy, knowledge, and skills. It's their contributions that unlocks scale.

It sounds simple enough, but it's actually a MASSIVE shift in mindset for most businesses.

There's strength in numbers. Companies that build engaged communities have access to exponentially more people who contribute to their mission and objectives. Whether it's your product, your marketing, your support, or any other part of your business, you can scale it by building and activating a community.

Community Is an Extension of Your Team

Traditional corporations are used to optimizing for control. They control the product, the brand, the messaging, the customer experience. To build community, companies have to learn to distribute control.

Historically, only employees would contribute, and customers would consume. Your marketing team does the marketing, your product team builds the product, your content team creates the content, your support team supports the customer. What community does is it extends the capacity and impact of each of those teams by organizing community members to contribute to the same kinds of projects and goals. That's the fundamental shift in how businesses function that's happening today. Anyone can contribute, if you'll let them.

To empower people means trusting them. And that isn't an easy pill to swallow for a lot of companies. It's one of the most common concerns I hear from the companies I've advised. They're afraid of a loss of quality, of misrepresentation of the brand, of things going off the rails if left to non-employees.

But consider this: by giving up some control, you remove a massive bottleneck to growth. Your community has the numbers. You can build a movement of people ready to collaborate and contribute in massive ways.

And you don't have to give up complete control. The idea is to create guide rails within which members will contribute. To host more local events, for example, companies will create a playbook that guides members on how to run an event, what the design requirements are, how to select speakers, the code of conduct, and anything else that they want to be consistent across the program. The local leaders then have creative freedom within those guide rails.

Phillippe Beaudette has built community teams at Wikipedia, Wikia, Reddit, and Atlassian. He once told me that his job, in any community position, is to "push out control as far as possible." He credits Jimmy Wales, the founder of Wikipedia, with teaching him this lesson. The key to Wikipedia's success is that the core team pushed control out to the edges of the community. Editors who create and edit the content on the site abide by consistent experiences, rules, and values that existed across the platform, but outside of those norms, had a great deal of autonomy.

In order to ensure that every member can experience the community in a way that's meaningful to them, you need to distribute control on the local level.

By local, I don't just mean geographically. Distributing control on the local level means you're putting control in the hands of the people who are closest to the problem you're trying to solve for. You're empowering the people most familiar with the needs and wants of the specific group of people you're trying to support.

That's the only way you can scale. Wikipedia put control in the hands of experts to develop articles on virtually every topic known to mankind. Reddit gives control to moderators to develop and manage subreddits, which cover hundreds of thousands of different interests. Duolingo gave their members control over creating language courses and organizing local events.

Every founder learns that the only way to grow their business is to delegate ownership to members of their team. If they can't let go of control, they become the bottleneck. To build community, you have to expand that same mentality beyond employees, and start distributing control to your customers

It doesn't have to be volunteer based. Some companies opt to hire for local leadership rather than working with volunteers. This is how Yelp, the restaurant and small business review website, runs their community. Once a city has a large enough audience, they'll place a full-time community manager in charge of that location. They create the local newsletter, host events, develop local partnerships, and handle everything specific to that city.

Other companies distribute control with financial incentives, allowing local leaders to earn profits through their work. This is how the TEDx program functions. If you organize a local TEDx event, you're responsible for running the entire event, and profits earned are yours to keep. Organizers are responsible for selling tickets, securing sponsorships, and managing the full budget for their programs. TED gives them a massive guide that walks them through everything they need to know to run an event. This creates a consistent experience across all TEDx events, while also giving the organizers a lot of autonomy to create a unique experience, select all the content, and make it more relevant on a local level.

That balance of setting consistent guide rails that everyone works within, while distributing control and decision-making power to your members, is critical for your community to sustainably scale.

The Power of Owning a Topic in People's Minds

Ultimately, what makes a business successful is the same thing that makes a community successful: Owning a topic in people's minds.

Building community is one of the most powerful ways to establish your brand as the most trusted leader in a category, or to get people bought into a category that you're working to create.

You want your community to be the first place people think of when they have a problem that needs solving in your category.

For millions of developers, when they get stuck on a problem, the first place they think of to go for help is Stack Overflow.

For millions of sales admins, when they have a problem, they turn to the Salesforce Trailblazer community.

For inbound marketers, there's no better resource than the Inbound conference and community hosted by Hubspot.

Humans are creatures of habit. When we find something that works, we do it again and again until neural pathways form and it becomes automatic.

Whenever we have a problem, and we think about where we can go for a solution, our brain will explore the options we already know and trust. You want your customers to find so much consistent value from your community that it becomes their go-to. You give them the security of knowing there's always a place they can turn.

And it will drive organic growth for your community, because it's an easy recommendation for your current members to make to others. It's how most people find out about our company and software. The majority of our growth comes from our members saying, "Oh you have a question about community strategy? You should totally check out CMX!"

Owning a topic in people's minds is quite simple (but not easy): you need to successfully solve their problem for them enough times that your community becomes the most efficient and trusted place they know of to get an answer, and they form a new habit. They need to feel confident that if they ask a question in your online community, they will get quality answers in a reasonable amount of time. They need to feel confident that if they show up to your event, the content and the attendees will be high quality, and they'll get the value they came for.

Then, whenever the thought pops into their head that they have a question or an idea around your topic, it will trigger them to think about your community, where they'll go first.

The One Thing They Can't Copy

One reason that community is becoming more important is that it's becoming much easier to build products, but it's always going to be very difficult to copy a community.

Anyone can rebuild your product today. Especially with the rise of "low-code" and "no-code" platforms, the ability to write code is no longer a requirement for starting a software company. Then there's the rapid rise of coding bootcamps and schools that are churning out more engineers every day. If you were counting on getting a head start on building technology as your competitive moat, you're likely to be disappointed.

Community, on the other hand, can't be copied, because community isn't software. Someone can copy the look, feel, and functionality
of your forum, but they'll lack the people, relationships, emotional
investment, and social identity that an established community has.

Community takes time to build, which can be a concern for companies who like to move fast and want to get results right away. A
realistic timeline for a community to drive value for a business is
more like 6–12 months. And it can take years for a community to
truly mature. But what that means is that it will take a competitor
just that long to build their own community. And if you've already
owned a topic in the mind of the consumer by building community,
it's very hard to get someone to leave a community they already feel
emotionally invested in.

The Salesforce Trailblazer community is a great example. When
you buy Salesforce software, you're not just getting the tools, you're
getting access to a massively valuable social and support network.
The community has become invaluable to many of its members, who
turn to the network for training and education. It's helped them grow
in their careers, get promotions and raises, and form deep relationships. That's something no other CRM software provider can provide
without spending years building the community the way the team
did at Salesforce.

There's already going to be a "switching cost" for anyone using
your product to use a different product. They've already gotten used
to your features and experience. Think about Apple and Microsoft
and how hard it is to get someone to switch computers. Community
adds an emotional layer to switching costs. To leave your product
would mean leaving their people, their relationships, and sacrificing
the social capital they've earned within your community. There's a
social cost to leaving your product.

Good for Business, Good for Humanity

We'll be talking a lot about the business value of community in this
book, but it's important not to discount the very real positive impact
that building community will have for your members and for the
world. It's the primary reason why I, and most people who build
communities, do this work.

Branded communities can be an engine for massive positive change in the world and in people's lives. A great company doesn't just look at profit as a measure of success. Truly great companies exist to have a positive impact on people's lives and make the world a better, more equitable, and more sustainable place.

Companies that invest in community purely for the business value and don't have authentic motivations to help people and create belonging will end up with a community that feels inauthentic, lacks resilience, and will struggle to scale their program because members just won't care that much about getting involved.

There are two things that every community program should focus on:

- How it creates value, belonging, and emotional safety for members
- How it creates value and measurable results for the business

You need to prioritize both (Figure 1.1).

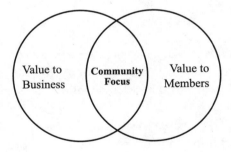

FIGURE 1.1

It can sometimes feel like businesses can't build authentic communities because they're so profit driven. If they always prioritize the bottom line over the needs of the people in the community, how can they claim to be truly community driven?

It's about taking a balanced approach. You have to make sure that you're building a growing and sustainable business so that you can put the proper resources into achieving your mission. And you have to make sure that you're always listening to and considering the needs of the people your business impacts.

In truth, a business is just another kind of community. And all communities need financial sustainability in order to exist and thrive.

Every business EVER had to make community a priority when it first started. The founders had to convince their first employees and customers to join them before they had product-market fit. They had to do "things that don't scale." They had to build relationships one at a time, and make people feel like they were part of something exciting … something larger than themselves.

The focus on community fades over time because the founders can't be as hands-on with each employee and each customer in the way they used to be. They become disconnected from the humans that make the business. That's where businesses go morally awry.

But if you look at the truly great companies, the ones that still lead with purpose even after they've gotten quite large, you'll find that all the elements of community are there: symbols, common language, shared sense of identity and purpose, communal spaces, an intentional culture, levels of leadership, etc. It's all there!

A community is a business.

A business is a community.

A great business focuses on serving people and building an incredible culture. And a great community figures out a way to be financially sustainable, so that it can continue to serve its members.

If a community runs out of money, it won't be helping anyone. The organizers won't be able to support themselves. They'll be under-resourced, spread thin, and stressed by the pressure of continuing to serve the community. Eventually they'll burn out, and the community will fade away. By figuring out how to make money, you have a chance to build a community that can sustainably support its members and leaders. I can't tell you how many times I've seen incredible communities fade away because the organizers just got burnt out by their lack of funds.

And if a business stops viewing itself as a community, and just looks at itself like a cold machine, well … we all know what happens then. Values go out the window. Cultures become toxic. Growth is pursued at all costs, lines are crossed, rules are broken, and the company's moral compass fades.

The most successful business leaders understand that their values and mission are why they exist, and profit is a means to achieve that impact. They understand that if they can truly make employees, partners, and customers feel valued, connected, collaborative, and empowered, that it has a real chance at reaching massive success.

And a thriving community understands that it needs to be a well-oiled machine, run professionally, and financially sustainable. Building community as a hobby is nice. But if you want to build a community sustainably, at scale, and expand way beyond your own abilities and resources, you need to look at it like a business.

Community is the job of every person on your team, not just the community team. The community team is responsible for organizing and facilitating spaces for members to connect with each other. But the product is solving a problem for a community, marketing is growing the community, and support is helping the community with their problems. It's ALL community.

Building belonging is no easy task. It takes a proper investment, the right team, and a genuine interest in helping your members. But if you do it right, you'll have a massive positive impact on your business's bottom line AND on the lives of everyone your business touches.

Notes

1. Tony Hsieh, "How I Did It: Zappos's CEO on Going to Extremes for Customers," Harvard Business Review, July 1, 2010, http://hbr.org/2010/07/how-i-did-it-zapposs-ceo-on-going-to-extremes-for-customers.

2. Carrie Melissa Jones, "Built to Belong: How the World's Top Brands Invest in Community," Gather Community Consulting, December 5, 2019, www.gathercommunityconsulting.com/blog/2019/12/2/built-to-belong-how-the-worlds-top-brands-invest-in-community-a-2019-trend-report.

3. David W. McMillan and David M. Chavis, "Sense of Community: A Definition and Theory," *Journal of Community Psychology* 14, no. 1 (January 1986): 6–23, https://onlinelibrary.wiley.com/doi/abs/10.1002/1520-6629%28198601%2914%3A1%3C6%3A%3AAID-JCOP2290140103%3E3.0.CO%3B2-I.

Chapter 2

The Fundamentals of Community Strategy

Now you hopefully have a high-level understanding of what it means for a business to build community. Building a true sense of community for your customers, or any other member type you're focusing on with your business, can unlock a massive source of passion and action that will help you scale your business. Community can help you create a new business category, or become the "go-to" resource in your category. It's the one thing competitors can't copy, and it's just a good thing to add to the world.

But what does that all mean for you and your business in practice? What does a community strategy look like? And is any of this business value measurable?

In this chapter, I'll teach you the simple structure you can use to map out your community strategy, and we'll go through The SPACES model, the go-to framework for defining exactly what objective community will drive for your business. We'll also talk about metrics, measuring the business value of community, and what the community investment journey looks like for every company.

The Three Levels of Community Strategy

If you want community to be something that your business makes a real investment in, and makes a core part of its strategy, then you have to be able to point to the measurable impact that community is having on your business.

Most companies when first investing in community focus entirely on engagement as a measure of success. They look at how many people are participating in their community, number of posts and comments, number of attendees, and other member engagement metrics. Community engagement on its own is not a measure of business value. It won't tell you anything about how community impacted the bottom line.

In the world of business, there are investments that are core to the business model and there are investments that are "for good" that don't contribute directly to the business model, but they're the right thing to do and are seen as charitable. As long as community lives in the purely "for good" side of a business, it will fail to get the resources it needs to be successful.

And our research shows that lack of resources is the #1 reason community programs fail at business.[1] Not lack of engagement. Lack of resources, rooted in an inability to prove the ROI.

The C-suite does care about building a healthy community and creating belonging for people. But they're not going to fully invest in community unless it's tied back to business impact. When push comes to shove, a business must earn more than it spends in order to survive. That is a rule that no business can break. Every CEO and leadership team is constantly making decisions about where to spend money and what to cut. They have to be diligent in making these decisions, because investing in things that don't contribute to the financial success of the organization increases the risk that the organization will fail.

And so when left with the decision of investing in something "for good" or investing in something that will help the business survive, survival always takes priority. You can't build community and do good in the world if you don't exist.

That doesn't mean that ROI is the only thing to measure! I don't want you to think that measuring community health and engagement isn't important.

The key is to communicate how community engagement is also achieving business goals that impact revenue and growth. They both matter. Business goals without a focus on building an authentic, healthy community will result in low engagement and trust. Community engagement goals without a focus on achieving business goals will result in an underfunded, undersupported community team.

Over the years we've developed a simple system for structuring and measuring your community strategy called the three levels of community strategy (Table 2.1).

TABLE 2.1   The Three Levels of Community Strategy

1. Business level	How your community program will drive revenue for your company.
2. Community level	How your community will grow and become more healthy and engaged over time.
3. Tactical level	The specific initiatives and improvements you work on in order to build a healthy, engaged community, and achieve the business outcomes.

At each of these levels, you'll have distinct goals and measures for tracking success. Altogether, the insights you gather through analytics, surveys, and interviews at each of these levels will tell the story of how the work you're doing week-to-week leads to a healthy and engaged community and drives measurable revenue for your business.

For example, here's how our goals at CMX can be broken down for a given quarter:

Business level
◆ Drive ticket and sponsorship sales for CMX Summit.
◆ Grow training and membership sales.
◆ Drive new leads and sales for our software product, Bevy.
◆ Drive customer retention and success for Bevy customers.

Community level
◆ Grow active membership in our online community spaces.
◆ Grow attendance and engagement at CMX Connect events.
◆ Grow active subscribers to the *CMX Weekly* newsletter.
◆ Increase the activation rate of new members joining the community.

Tactical level

- Update our email newsletter design to increase click rates and drive more community engagement.
- Create a new onboarding experience for CMX Connect hosts to increase the success rate for new hosts to launch their first events.
- Launch a new content campaign in the Facebook group to increase engagement and activate lurkers.
- Send personal invites to our events to our top 100 target accounts.
- Add CMX Academy trainings to Bevy customer onboarding.

Each of these goals will have measures attached to them so we can track our success.

You can see how some of the tactics and initiatives we focus on will (hopefully) drive increased community engagement and health, and some are specifically focused on driving revenue through community programs and content.

We'll spend the rest of this book going through frameworks, tips, and tricks to help you be successful at each of the three levels of community strategy.

We'll start with the end in mind, identifying the business outcomes we aim to achieve with community.

The SPACES Model: The Six Business Outcomes of Community

The SPACES model was built by our team to help businesses understand the different types of measurable outcomes that are driven by communities. This simple framework has been used by thousands of companies to identify the key business objectives and revenue drivers for their communities.

It doesn't matter if your product IS a community, or if you're building a community alongside another product or service that you sell.

All companies can apply the SPACES model to identify the specific objectives that community can drive.

All community programs will drive at least one, but often multiple, of these six business outcomes:

1. **Support:** *Customer service and support.* The goal is to improve customer support and satisfaction, and reduce support costs by empowering members to answer questions and solve problems for each other.

2. **Product:** *Innovation, feedback, and R&D.* The goal is to accelerate innovation and improve your product offering by creating spaces for members to share their feedback and discuss ideas that they'd like to see you apply to your product.

3. **Acquisition:** *Growth, marketing, and sales.* The goal is to increase brand awareness, grow market share, and drive SEO, traffic, and leads, by hosting online and offline community spaces and/or empowering ambassadors to create content, organize events, and advocate on your behalf.

4. **Contribution:** *Collaboration and crowdsourcing.* The goal is to motivate and accelerate the contribution of content, products, and services on your platform, marketplace, or social network. This is a common objective for companies whose core offering is a community, or is inherently social.

5. **Engagement:** *Customer experience, retention, and loyalty.* The goal is to increase customer retention, average contract value, and customer satisfaction by giving customers a sense of belonging and organizing engaging and valuable community experiences.

6. **Success:** *Customer success and advancement.* The goal is to make customers more successful at using your product, resulting in increased spend, retention, and satisfaction, by empowering them to teach each other, help each other skill up, and grow in their careers.

In this book, mostly use "customers" as the primary member type that communities focus on, but you can apply the SPACES model and everything discussed in this book to any identity that a business interacts with, including users, sellers, employees, partners, alumni, volunteers, donors … whoever your member type is.

For example, some community teams are focused internally on building community and belonging for their employees. Here's how you'd apply the SPACES model to employees:

Support: Empower employees to answer questions and solve problems for each other.

Product: Create spaces for employees to discuss how to improve the product as well as company processes, culture, and messaging.

Acquisition: Create a program that empowers employees to recruit new employees and customers, and helps them become stronger advocates and thought leaders.

Contribution: Create opportunities for employees to contribute content in their area of expertise, or have the opportunity to get involved in projects outside of their normal realm of work.

Engagement: Create community experiences that make employees feel a stronger sense of belonging, give them social value, and increase the likelihood that they'll stick around as an employee for the long run.

Success: Empower employees to teach classes for each other, help each other skill up, and grow in their careers.

The SPACES model can also apply to different kinds of organizations like nonprofits or political initiatives. Just swap out "customer" with "donors" or "volunteers" or "voters" and you can see how it will apply.

Support: Empower volunteers to answer questions and solve problems for each other.

Product: Create spaces for volunteers and contributors to share their ideas for how your organization can have a bigger impact and improve its initiatives.

Acquisition: Empower volunteers to speak on behalf of your organization, advocate for the movement, and recruit new volunteers.

Contribution: Empower your volunteers to contribute their stories and ideas in public-facing content, or allow them to contribute their time/services to support the people you're trying to impact.

Engagement: Create community experiences that help volunteers connect with each other more deeply and feel like they belong to an incredible community so that they stay involved longer.

Success: Empower volunteers to teach each other how to be more successful in their volunteer work, and help them skill up in areas that will help them in their overall career.

In Chapter 1 we spoke about how community is an extension of your team. You can see how the six areas of the SPACES model are six of the essential areas of any business. Each one likely already has a dedicated team focused on that area in your business, and community can amplify the bandwidth and impact of that team.

Community isn't meant to replace your existing programs. It's meant to enhance and accelerate it. Look at your support program and think about how community can amplify the work that they're doing by empowering experts to contribute. Look at your marketing programs and think about how community can accelerate growth by activating your biggest advocates.

Let's explore each part of the model in a little more detail and go through some examples.

Support

Customer support is how you answer questions and solve problems for your customers. Community-driven customer support is any program where you're empowering customers to answer questions and solve problems for each other.

Support communities are the most traditional form of community programs. It's a big part of the "self-service" approach, where customers can help themselves by finding answers to their questions in help documents created by support staff or community members.

Support forums have become quite popular online today. Apple still uses a support forum as the first line of response for customers to get support with their products. Cisco, Wordpress, Spotify, Fitbit, Google – name any brand, and there's a good chance they have a support forum.

The purpose of a Support community is to create a space where your customers can answer questions for each other. They're mostly online, forum-based, and tend to be used for more technical products where there are a lot of specific questions.

The members of these groups are experts who know your product inside and out, and are motivated to help other customers with their challenges.

If you're running a program like this, your goal is typically going to be to reduce support costs, improve support efficiency, and improve customer satisfaction.

A support forum can look very different from other community spaces and have different engagement metrics. For example, if your community is all about facilitating interesting discussions, you'll generally want more comments, not less. But in a support forum, it's all about optimizing for the best answer. More answers isn't necessarily better, and can result in more confusion for the customer trying to find a solution. The poster will often be asked to select the "best answer" to make it easier for other customers with the same problem to find the solution.

All communities will have a distribution of user engagement, from passive to active to power users (more on that later), but this will be especially true in support forums. It's likely that a small percentage of participants on the forum will actually feel a strong sense of belonging and will answer the majority of the questions. The extreme majority of people coming to the forum are just looking for a solution to their problem, not a social experience.

But for the members who are answering lots of questions and putting in the time to support other members, you can bet they feel a strong sense of purpose and belonging. The actual belonging building efforts will be focused on these contributors, and for everyone else, it's all about optimizing your operations to make sure they can find the most relevant information in the right amount of time.

That doesn't mean you shouldn't prioritize the more passive members of your community. Caty Kobe, who has led support community programs at Square, OpenTable, and Get Satisfaction, often talks about the importance of the "logged-out" experience in support communities. "A lot of the people participating in these spaces shouldn't even have to sign up or log in to get the information they need. They just need the solution to their problem," says Kobe.

These kinds of community spaces are really powerful sources of information for your team about what pain points customers are dealing with, and any potential issues that exist as you continue to update and chance your product. "For every one customer who complains, there are 26 customers who stay silent," says Kobe. Community can be a canary in the proverbial coal mine, warning you of much larger issues to come before they wreak havoc for your brand.

A common fear for companies is that if they open up a space for customers to share their problems, that it will be really negative and toxic. To that, I always remind them that any negativity that people feel toward your product is already being shared, just not in spaces where you have access and influence. It's much better to be able to own the space where these conversations are happening, to hear what people are saying, and be able to proactively respond. Kobe always recommends taking any heated conversations offline, "Ask the member to chat over email or phone where you can address their concerns one-on-one, or even escalate to a senior customer support agent to address sensitive situations."

Even in the most negative communities, over time you can turn the corner and develop a culture of positivity and optimism by continuing to show up, make your customers feel heard, and address their concerns with honesty and transparency.

Product

Successful product development is all about listening to customers, doing research and development to understand their needs so you can innovate and stay ahead of the curve. By creating spaces where your community can share feedback, insights, and ideas in a social setting, your company can observe those conversations and identify the most important needs.

These community programs can take the form of small groups, like the Lyft Driver Advisory Council (DAC), which started out as a group of seven representatives that Lyft brought in to share their perspective on big product decisions. Today there are over a hundred members in the DAC. These drivers are chosen from different regions in the United States, and they are representative voices of the community. Lyft pays them an annual stipend for their time and contributions, and they rotate out the ambassadors every year.

These programs can also take the form of big online spaces with thousands of members adding ideas, voting, and commenting, like the Xbox Ideas space where customers share, vote on, and comment on ideas and feedback in an online space.

If you're running a program like this, you're likely going to measure the number of ideas that are submitted, accepted, and applied to the product. Some companies take it further and measure the impact that these new features have on revenue. You can also measure the impact this work has on support costs: Does the new feature also address an existing issue that was driving contact volume? Were a lot of customers calling in with the feature request itself?

Truth-be-told, this is one of the hardest objectives to tie directly back to revenue. How do you measure the value of a piece of feedback? What's the value of innovation? Sometimes companies can estimate the specific cost savings in research and development, like Techsmith, who found that crowdsourcing ideas from their community saved them $500,000.[2]

Either way, these kinds of communities undoubtedly drive massive impact for companies who can incorporate the voice of their customers into their product development process. They have a constant source of feedback and insight from people on the ground. Gathering qualitative feedback from your product team about how the community has helped them make decisions can make a compelling case for investing in these programs. Product teams absolutely love having an engaged community that they can always turn to for feedback.

Product focused community programs also help earn the trust of a customer-base, who will feel like they're being listened to, and that they have an impact on the product and business. A key to building thriving communities is making people feel ownership in the process. When you launch a feature that they recommended, they'll take great pride in that feature, and will become a bigger advocate for it.

Acquisition

Community was built into the fabric of Lululemon from its very early days. Store managers were empowered to be community organizers, and to identify community leaders in their local markets. These leaders, who were often fitness instructors, coaches, and yoga teachers, were made into official "Lululemon Ambassadors" and could organize their own events and experiences under the Lululemon brand. As a result, customers learned about their products not from traditional marketing and advertising, but from other customers who were passionate about the Lululemon brand and products.

Acquisition-focused community programs are all about spreading brand awareness and moving people along the sales funnel, from leads to prospect, to opportunities, and ultimately to become customers.

These can be any program where you're connecting and empowering your most loyal customers to organize and advocate on your behalf. They can also be community spaces that you make available to the public so people can discover your community, which leads them to learn about your products and offerings.

These programs are run both online and offline. They're often content-driven, with the advocates creating content or speaking on your behalf. They can also be event driven, where ambassadors organize experiences in-person and virtually to gather new and existing community members.

These kinds of "distributed leadership" programs where the company identifies local ambassadors to serve as chapter leaders who can host events for other customers in their region are becoming extremely popular and can be highly effective. The chapter leader gets approval to represent the brand, they're given a playbook for how to run their events, and the company supports them with resources, training, and benefits. We'll talk more about these kinds of programs in Chapter 4.

Sometimes an acquisition community is less about ambassadors, and looks more like a standard community built around a common interest. The goal, for the business, is to create a space where their potential audience can gather to discuss something they're passionate about. These communities can become a "first touch" in the buyer's journey, or become a way of consistently engaging active leads.

A great example of this kind of community is Culture Amp, the employee feedback and surveying tool. Culture Amp created a public-facing community called "People Geeks" with this purpose. The goal was to bring together anyone who's working on employee engagement to talk about the industry, give them a ton of value and earn their trust. Now when that person learns about Culture Amp's brand and products, they'll already trust them and value their leadership in the market.

Ironclad did the same thing for their target audience, in-house legal professionals. They started organizing dinners and events focused on engaging key prospects in their pipeline and giving them a chance to talk to loyal customers in a communal setting. Jason Boehmig, Ironclad's CEO, shared that its community program has already driven over $8 million in annual recurring revenue for the fast-growing startup.

Acquisition is an area that a lot of community teams don't lean into nearly enough. Understandably, they're afraid of making their community too sales-y and losing trust with community members.

You should absolutely not come in hard with a cold-sale in a community, certainly not if you haven't established trust already. But you should look at every interaction someone has with your community as a touchpoint in the sales journey.

Mary Thengvall is the author of *The Business Value of Developer Relations* and teaches companies about the concept of community-qualified leads (CQLs). The same way marketing teams have marketing-qualified leads (MQLs) and sales teams have sales-qualified leads (SQLs), community engagement is a very strong method of qualifying leads. When someone attends your event, or participates in your online community, that's data you can use to better understand how strong of a relationship you have with that person, and how strong of a fit your product is for them. You can see the topics that they engage in to better understand the challenges they might need help with. This will help your marketing and sales team better understand who to focus on, and how to authentically solve their problems.

For our own product Bevy, it's rare that a company becomes a customer who hasn't engaged in the CMX community in some way. It's very likely that they've attended an event and have multiple people participating in our community before they ever get on the phone with a sales representative. Our sales reps love hearing that, because they know that there's already established trust. That makes their job a lot easier.

There's absolutely a wrong way to use community to drive sales. But when it's done right, and authentically, it can become your company's strongest growth engine.

Contribution

The internet is, at its core, a collaborative environment. Some of today's biggest businesses and most popular websites are open spaces that anyone can contribute to. Airbnb is a space where members can add their homes for rent. Wikipedia is a space where people add and edit their knowledge. Google's tablet and smartphone apps are developed by independent businesses and individuals on the Android platform.

Any time you see a platform where the content is being generated by members, including social networks, marketplaces, open-source products, and collaborative consumption networks, there's likely a community program sitting at its core.

Take Udemy, for example. Today, Udemy is one of the largest online learning platforms in the world, and all the classes are created by members of the community. Back in 2012, Udemy was growing very quickly but wanted to improve its instructor activation and retention rate. While some teachers would quickly become successful on the platform, many instructors would get stuck and leave before ever getting their class up. I was brought in to help them take a community approach to solving the problem.

We found that launching a class on Udemy wasn't very easy. An instructor had to develop curriculum, record all the videos, learn how to use Udemy to upload the content, launch the course, and be able to market and sell it. There are a lot of points along that journey where an instructor can get stuck and drop off. Udemy had full-time staff dedicated to helping instructors get set up, but it was becoming expensive and hard to scale.

The competitive advantage of Udemy is that it can launch more quality classes faster than any other platform by letting anyone teach a class on the platform. So requiring full-time staff to work with each instructor was a major risk. It was a bottleneck that could ruin the business model.

By taking a community approach and creating a space for instructors to support and onboard each other, they would no longer need full-time staff to work with every new instructor. And instead of just feeling like they were a user of a platform, instructors would feel welcomed into a community of instructors who shared a lot of their same goals and challenges.

The Udemy instructor community was born. Today, the Udemy Instructor Community has over 10,000 instructors connecting and supporting each other with feedback and advice. Udemy's business revolves around course sales, and the community team is directly influencing the bottom line by helping instructors become more successful at selling their courses on the platform.

You can find similar programs at Airbnb with their host and superhost communities, Wikipedia with their editor communities, Ethereum with their contributor forums, Google with their Google Developer Groups, Yelp with the Yelp Elite, and pretty much any business where contributors make the platform tick.

The truth with all open platforms is that a very small percentage of users are going to generate most of the content. Some studies show that 80 percent of the content will be created by 20 percent of the users. And, at a big enough size, it's possible that only 1 percent of your members will be consistent, active contributors. That's why it's so important that you make your contributors successful. A small group can have outsized impact on the rest of your business.

Engagement

Community programs can be massively effective at fueling customer retention. When customers feel like they're truly part of a community, and not just transactional consumers, they're much less likely to switch to a competitor. They're getting social value as well as practical value.

Engagement is the most popular objective for community programs, with 33 percent of companies reporting that this is the primary goal of their community.[3] It's often what we think of when a business says "our community."

I spoke earlier about Duolingo and the thousands of events hosted by their community every month. These events are hosted because they wanted to give their learners an opportunity to connect with each other and advance their speaking skills. So Duolingo empowered members to organize gatherings to practice their languages live, in-person. As a result, learners continue to get value beyond just the courses themselves, and continue to be engaged with the platform.

A lot of community programs achieve multiple goals and will drive both engagement and acquisition. Culture Amp's People Geek community, for example, is built both for customers and for their broader industry. They create spaces for customers to support each other, and connect customers with noncustomers, to fuel both engagement and acquisition.

One challenge that even most mature community programs have is getting the data necessary to measure the business value of their Engagement community. Does attending your community events, and participating in your digital community, increase the lifetime value of your customer?

In order to do this, you need to be able to connect your community data to your customer data. Most companies use a customer relationship management (CRM) tool to track their customer data. We discussed in Acquisition the concept of community-qualified leads and how you can track touchpoints with leads and prospects. The same is true for existing customers. You can track community engagement and touchpoints to see how it's playing a role in the customer experience and renewal rates.

Our research found that only one third of companies are able to connect their community data to their customer data.[4] Not the worst, but for community teams to be able to continue to grow and get buy-in, this is a non-negotiable. Without the data, you can't say for sure that community is having an impact on your business, and it will be very difficult to justify increasing budget in community.

Success

Community-driven success programs are where you're empowering and facilitating education created by your members for your members. The goal is to help them become more efficient and capable at using your product, and to help them grow in their career through improving skills and strategic abilities.

This takes customer support, which can tend to be more reactive and very product focused, to a more proactive approach with a bigger focus on improving skills and strategic abilities.

The Salesforce Trailblazer community is a great example of this kind of program. Salesforce provides its customers with tons of training, classes, mentorship programs, and other resources to help them better use Salesforce, and to develop skills that are important for their career.

These programs are so powerful because they communicate to customers that it isn't just about selling them more products. It's a partnership. And the business is investing in helping them grow their careers. Now, if a customer joins a new company that isn't currently a Salesforce customer, they'll be much more likely to recommend Salesforce, and they'll still be engaged with the brand.

Google's G2G program is another great example of a community-driven success program. It's an internal community program for employees (which for Google is the size of a small country!). Every Google office sets up a team of volunteer "Office Leads" who help facilitate educational programs where Google employees can teach classes to each other. Classes can range from coding workshops, to yoga, to art, to public speaking. It helps employees learn skills that are relevant not only to their job but also for their life and overall career.

The best part about success programs is that by making your customers into experts and investing in their career, you'll undoubtedly create more passionate advocates who then want to give back to the community and company. You'll create a whole new wave of leaders who will teach classes, host events, support other customers, and invite others into your community. Invest in the success of your community members, and they'll be motivated to invest in your success.

Metrics and the Attribution Challenge

Each area of the SPACES model represents a goal that you can try to achieve, and each goal has some commonly used metrics you can use for tracking your success in that objective. Table 2.2 shows a few recommendations for each one.

These are just a few recommendations of metrics you can use for each objective. You should choose metrics that provide insight into the specific goals of your community team and organization.

Not all of these are very easy to track or to connect to community engagement data. Sometimes, you'll be able to show correlation but not causation. For example, the Sephora Beauty Talk community team found that members who participate in the forum spend two times more than their average customer. And their power members spend 10 times more than their average customer. Now, are they spending more because of the community? Or are they participating in the community more because they're more invested as a customer? Hard to say.

What if someone comes to your event and then buys your product. Did the event cause them to buy your product? Or were they going to buy already? The data alone won't give you the answer without follow-up surveys and interviews.

But community isn't alone in this challenge. The truth is, there are very few things in business that you can say with certainty is a direct cause and effect.

In marketing, someone might read an article you published, get a referral from another customer, see an advertisement, and download your report before ultimately deciding to sign up for a demo or buy your product. We don't know which one of those touchpoints really motivated the person to take a buying action. We just know that there was a "first touch," a "last touch," and that these were all touchpoints that likely contributed to their decision.

Community is another touchpoint, and it's a damn powerful one at that. You don't need community to be the single thing that made a person decide to buy your product, to renew a contract, to give you a high customer satisfaction score, or accomplish any of the goals in the SPACES model. You do want to be able to show if and when community was a touchpoint on the journey to that outcome. Then

TABLE 2.2   The SPACES model.

	Goal	Metrics
Support	Improve customer satisfaction and save on support costs.	◆ Support for cost savings ◆ Reduced customer churn ◆ Improved customer service experience ratings
Product	Improve products with feedback and insights from the community.	◆ Revenue generated from community-sourced ideas ◆ Reduced R&D time and costs ◆ Decisions influenced by community feedback
Acquisition	Acquire new leads, customers or users.	◆ New customers, members, or users acquired through community ◆ Pipeline (community-qualified leads, prospects and opportunities) generated ◆ Increased sales conversion rate and reduced sales cycle time
Contribution	Drive quality contributions to a collaborative or social platform or marketplace.	◆ Contributor onboarding success rate ◆ Contributor actions (posts, sales, listings, etc.) and retention ◆ Revenue per successful contributor
Engagement	Improve customer satisfaction through community experiences.	◆ Customer lifetime value (CLV) ◆ Customer satisfaction score (CSAT) ◆ Net promoter score (NPS)
Success	Drive product adoption and customer expansion.	◆ Feature adoption rate ◆ Increased average contract value ◆ Reduced onboarding time

you'll be able to say with confidence that community is meaningfully driving growth and retention.

Finding Your Community Focus

It's important to focus on just one or two primary objectives for your community program when you're first getting started and your community team is small. But this is rarely what happens.

Every time I teach a workshop, just about everyone in the room finds that they're focusing on many or all of these objectives. It's common because most of the time when a company hires a community professional and launches a community program, they don't know why they're doing it other than "community seems important." The community becomes a solution in search of a problem.

And because community as a profession is so new, and still often hard to measure, the community person wants to show that community can create as much value as possible! So they choose a number of different objectives that they can impact for the business. "Look at all of these amazing ways community can drive value for sales, product, support, and marketing!" they'd proclaim in their slide deck, presenting to the executives who tasked them with coming up with the strategy. "LET'S INVEST IN ALL THE SPACES!"

This, my friends, is a recipe for disaster.

The community team owning this program is set up to fail. They become accountable to six different objectives. Each objective requires working with a different team in the business (product, support, marketing, customer, etc.) so now they have to coordinate communications and manage expectations of basically every group in the company.

On top of that, each objective requires different metrics to determine success. That means they have to identify the right data, which likely lives in many different tools and databases, access that data, connect it all back to the community, and report on it regularly.

Each objective then has different tools and software that specialize in a specific kind of interaction and objective. For example, some tools are much more optimized for support communities, and won't be set up well for acquisition.

And each objective also requires organizing different groups of members! Because the members who are motivated and capable of being an expert answering questions in a support forum may be very different from the members who are motivated and capable of being ambassadors and hosting events, or the members who have lots of useful product feedback!

You get the point. By focusing on six objectives, the community team is essentially doing the job of six teams. (Remember, community is an extension of your team!)

They're spreading themselves way too thin to be able to have a meaningful impact on any one of those objectives. And when the day comes that they have to report on the value they've driven for the organization, it's going to be really difficult for them to tell a clear, concise story, with data, about how community helped the business grow.

So please, find your focus!

Prioritize the areas that are most important for your business today. If your company is in a growth phase, and leadership is banging the growth drum, then that's the key value you should prioritize with your community. That's the objective that you should be measuring and reporting on first. If your business is making customer retention a huge priority since you've been losing too many recently, then make Engagement, Success, or Support your priority. It'll be much easier to get buy-in and feel confident that community is impacting the business.

Here's the thing: the community will organically still drive value in the other areas whether or not you've made it a priority. Let's say you host a community conference with the primary goal of attracting new customers (Acquisition). There's a good chance you'll also ...

◆ Have a booth where customers can ask product questions and share their feedback with your product team (Support and Product).

◆ Invite community members to contribute content and speak on stage (Contribution).

◆ Invite customers to attend and form new relationships to increase retention (Engagement).

◆ Have lots of content specifically focused on helping your customers be more successful at using your product and teaching them skills that are important for their careers (Success).

The measure of success for this event will be around acquisition. The story you want to be able to tell after the event is that it drove new leads and helped close customers. But that doesn't mean that it won't also drive other areas of the SPACES model. It's just not what you're focused on and accountable for. It's icing on the cake.

After you've proven one objective out, you can point to the organic value that it's driving for other parts of the business and launch a new community initiative.

This is what Erica Kuhl did when she was tasked with starting the community program at Salesforce. Deep down, she believed that the most valuable aspect of community for their company would be in product, but she knew that she'd have a hard time getting buy-in. So she started by focusing on something she knew she could measure.

"I started with something very tangible, which was focused on getting questions answered by peers," Kuhl explained. I tracked questions answered by non-Salesforce and cost offset for support. I also focused on marketing specific outcomes and metrics since I was in the marketing department – such as speakers sourced, quotes and testimonials, and identifying advocates."

By proving that community could reduce support costs, and impact marketing initiatives, she was able to get buy-in from execs to start building community programs focused on product innovation. "Our next focus was launching the IdeaExchange where community members would share their product feedback requests and vote on their top ideas. This was one of the programs that proved that community could drive higher product adoption."

Today, community teams exist in many of Salesforce's different product organizations, and community is driving value in every area of the SPACES model, all organized through a centralized community team. If Kuhl tried to boil the ocean on day one and achieve all of these objectives, she would have had a much harder time getting buy in. She stayed focused and chose a value that the she knew she could measure. It's no surprise she became one of the first legitimate VPs of Community in the industry.

Growth Engines vs. Cost Centers

Too many businesses still look at community as a cost center, and just only at cost savings as proof of ROI.

The most clear-cut way to drive value for most businesses is going to be bringing in new revenue. That's why the community teams that are able to prove that community doesn't only save money, but brings in new revenue, are going to be much more successful.

To understand how community drives growth, you want to be able to see exactly when and how leads, prospects, and customers interacted with the community over time.

Say you want to acquire 100 new customers through your community.

Now you need to sit down with your sales or marketing team and find out what their conversion funnel looks like.

A really simple sales funnel looks like this: Audience > Lead > Opportunity > Sale

So you have to find three ratios:

1. Percentage of audience that converts to leads
2. Percentage of leads that convert to opportunities
3. Percentage of opportunities that convert to sales

Let's say that 10 percent of your audience converts to leads, 25 percent of leads convert to opportunities, and 50 percent of opportunities convert to sales.

If you need to get 100 sales, that means you need 200 opportunities, which means you need 800 leads, which means you need 8,000 people in the audience.

Great! Now you have your goal. You need to get 8,000 people to engage in your community in order to hit the goal. At least that's your hypothesis. Is it perfect? No. Business never is. But this will give you a baseline to work with.

If you're running an event-based community program, you'll want to make sure you can get 8,000 attendees by the deadline, and ensure you're collecting the right data from attendees so that your marketing team can qualify them as leads.

Let's say you get 25 attendees at each local event, on average. Now you know how many events you'll need the community to host in order to hit your goal: 320 events.

And if your local chapters host an average of 10 events per year, you'll need 32 chapters up and running for a full year to hit your goal.

Roll up your sleeves; it's time to start recruiting chapter leaders!

Your online community can work much in the same way. You'll need to get 8,000 people to sign up for the community and collect the right data from them at sign up, if you don't already have it.

Now, you can also work community more deeply into the growth strategy by making it a data point in lead qualification, going back to Mary Thengvall's concept of CQLs. For example, you can look at the number of events attended as a signal for how qualified a lead is. If someone has only attended one event, that's a lower signal. If they've attended three or more events, they become a more qualified lead, because it shows that the person is more engaged with our community and brand.

Same for online. Someone who just joined the community but never participated may not be a quality lead. But someone who logs in regularly, and maybe even posts or responds to posts regularly, is more deeply engaged, making them a stronger lead.

You can build community-based lead qualifications into your CRM, so your marketing and sales team can always see who's engaged in the community when prioritizing who to focus on.

Now, at the end of each quarter and each year, you can generate a really simple, compelling report about how community impacted the business. You'll be able to say things like:

- This quarter the community brought in 300 new leads, which led to 75 opportunities and 40 sales, a total of $800,000 in annual revenue.
- The community has now brought in a total of $2,100,000 in annual revenue this year.
- 30 percent of our customers are also engaged in our community, an increase from 21 percent six months ago.
- Customers who are engaged in our community were 23 percent more likely to renew than customers who are not engaged in the community.

Or you can break down the makeup of the community membership, and say, "Of the 8,000 members who participated in our community this quarter:

35 percent were new leads

20 percent were qualified leads

10 percent were opportunities

35 percent were existing customers

This gives the team a clear image of how community is serving as a valuable touchpoint at each stage of the customer journey.

Choosing a Measurement Framework

When it comes to putting the three levels of community strategy into practice, and setting clear annual, quarterly, and monthly goals and objectives, you don't have to reinvent the wheel.

Business has been around for a long time, and a lot of smart people have attempted to tackle the problem of how to efficiently set goals and metrics that will lead to a successful business.

I used to be overwhelmed by all the different words and systems that people use. OKRs, 4DX, V2MOMs ... businesses love their acronyms and abbreviations, don't they?

After using all three of those systems at different points in my career, I discovered that pretty much every strategic framework is fundamentally the same. Seriously ... they're all just different words for the same exact concepts. I'll explain.

All strategic frameworks aim to take a big nebulous goal and make it more specific. They all do this with three elements:

1. *The goal* you're trying to achieve
2. *The measures* that will tell you if you've achieved that goal
3. *The actions* you'll take in order to achieve the goal

That's it, it's that simple! Let's look at those three strategic frameworks and how they fit.

◆ OKRs were popularized in the book *Measure What Matters* by John Doerr. There are three pieces to OKRs:
  • Objectives (the goal)
  • Key Results (the measures)
  • Initiatives (the actions)
◆ 4DX is short for *Four Disciplines of Execution,* a book by Jim Huling, Chris McChesney, and Sean Covey. There are three elements to 4DX:
  • Wildly important goal (the goal)
  • Lag measures (the measures)
  • Lead measures (the actions)

◆ V2MOM is the system that was popularized by Marc Benioff at Salesforce and explained in his book *Behind the Cloud*. There are five elements to V2MOMs, which includes our core three elements with two added:
  • Vision (the goal)
  • Values
  • Measures (the measures)
  • Obstacles
  • Methods (the actions)

At Salesforce, whenever they do strategic planning, they make sure to also incorporate their company values, and talk through obstacles that might prevent them from achieving their goal. Great additions, but we can see the core framework is consistent with those three elements.

Your company may already have a standard framework that everyone uses. If it doesn't, then feel free to pick one and read one of those books. They're all great.

With a strategic framework in place, you're ready to start planning, measuring, and executing. Every successful community team I've spoken to uses one of these systems, or something similar, to guide their programs.

Let's look at a real world example. I mentioned Ironclad earlier and how their community program drove over $8 million in annual recurring revenue. CEO Jason Beehmig shared at our conference in 2019 that "50 percent of our revenue is touched by the community."

This success is largely the result of the strategy developed by Ironclad's community lead, Vera Devera. She shared with me the goals and measures she uses at each of the three levels (business, community, and tactical) of her community strategy. (I've changed some of their numbers that they couldn't share publicly.)

For Ironclad, the business level of their community strategy looks like this:

◆ *Goal:* Grow sales pipeline each quarter.
◆ *Measures:* Pipeline touchpoints, "Logos Won."
◆ *Actions:* Host valuable events to build trust and authority with prospects.

The actions from your business-level strategy will become your goals for the community level of your strategy.

The community level of Ironclad's strategy looks like this:

◆ *Goal:* Host valuable events to build trust and authority with prospects.
◆ *Measures:* Five events hosted, 75 target accounts in attendance, NPS of 85, or higher.
◆ *Actions:* Send very personalized email invites to target accounts and improve the email communication flows before and after events.

The actions from the community level of your strategy become you tactical-level goals:

◆ *Goals:* Send personalized email invites and improve the email communication flows before and after events.
◆ *Measures:* Send invites to 150 target accounts, 75 percent open rate on invitation emails, 90 percent open rate on even communications emails, and 75 percent response rate on post-event surveys.
◆ *Actions:* Research the top 150 accounts to understand their specific needs, and get feedback on new drafts for email communications.

So you can see how you start with the end in mind. What is the business goal? From there, you lay out how you'll build community that achieves those goals. You keep getting more specific until you know exactly what you're focusing on this week, month, or quarter, and how that work ultimately impacts the community and the business.

Devera tracks every event and is constantly iterating to make sure the events are both valuable to customers and positively affect buy-in for their business goals. "I track everything using Salesforce and Bevy to see how community influences sales. If certain kinds of events aren't having a big enough impact, we'll do those less, and focus on events that have a bigger impact." She knows that there are an infinite amount of experiences she can organize for her community, but by prioritizing the ones that have the most impact on the business, she can ensure that her community program will keep getting the buy-in, and budget, it deserves.

Not everything you do needs to impact revenue. It shouldn't. If you're only connecting your members to make money, you'll end up with a cold, inauthentic community. A lot of a community team's work won't directly impact revenue. But by understanding the business impact that your community must achieve from the outset, you can ensure that your program is helping both your members and your business achieve their goals.

The Community Investment Journey

As we move into the practical "how to" part of the book that will help you build a true community, it's important to note where you are in your community investment journey.

Some of you reading this book will be pretty far along in your community journey. You might already have spaces you're hosting, an engaged member base, and a good foundation of community.

Some of you might be building a community from scratch. If you're building community for a company, maybe you're part of a brand new startup, or your business is well-established and just hasn't done much to build community yet.

Where you are in your journey will impact your community strategy. Your priorities for managing a brand new community will look very different than the priorities for an established community. New communities won't have established norms, members won't yet feel a strong sense of community, and your operations will be more minimal. More established communities will be more complex in their systems, and have a lot of growth and engagement happening organically since members already have a sense of community and have developed habits of contribution.

To help you better understand the journey of investing in community, and figure out how to focus your time based on the stage you're at, I like to use the community life cycle. The concept of a community life cycle was first developed by Alicia Iriberri and Gondy Leroy in their research on online communities.[5] Today, you can find many different versions of the life cycle concept online.

When I teach the community life cycle to companies, I explain it like the growth of a tree. As you can see in Figure 2.1, there are four stages.

1. *Seed.* The community is first started and needs a lot of love and care to keep it alive.
2. *Growth.* There's community-market fit and the community starts to organically grow and engage.
3. *Maturity.* The community becomes well-established, with clear norms and leadership structure.
4. *Pollination.* The community becomes so large that it breaks out into peripheral or subcommunities, that become their own seed stage communities and move through the cycle while still under the umbrella of the broader, more mature community.

The Seed Stage

This is the very beginning of your community's life. It's just a seedling. Its chance of survival is low and it needs a lot of care and attention if it's going to survive this fragile phase. Your community won't drive much business value in the seed stage. You need a mature tree to bear fruit. In these early days, focus less on business value and more on building the foundation of community.

The seed is essentially an idea. It's a belief that there's a group of people who don't yet have a space to call their own. The community doesn't yet have a strong identity, set of norms or beliefs, or formal structures. It's a small group exploring the potential of community.

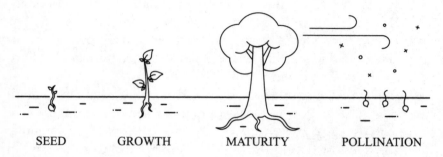

SEED   GROWTH   MATURITY   POLLINATION

FIGURE 2.1

Today, in the internet era, millions of communities are created because the barrier to entry is so low, and people can connect with anyone else in the world. You can start a Facebook group in just a few clicks. But most communities don't get off the starting block, past the seed stage. It might seem easy to build community when you're looking at established communities as models, but it takes an extraordinary effort to get them successfully off the ground.

The community builder must show up consistently, time-and-time again, even when no one else shows up, or engagement is slow. You must keep at it, failing, learning, and adapting over and over again. You might be starting 90 percent of the discussions yourself.

The things you want to focus on in the early days of a community are very different from what you'll focus on at later stages. You'll never learn how to build a new community by looking at existing communities just like you'll never learn how to make a new startup successful by copying well-established companies. The successful communities you see today looked very different when they first started. If you're starting a new community, then look at how other communities started, not how they look in their mature stage today.

Sometimes, communities blast through this phase. The circumstances were perfect, people were craving community, and the community went from the seed stage straight to growth. This happens a lot with political movements, protests, or riots where there was already a lot of built-up energy around a topic, and a spark that mobilizes people in what seems like an instant. It can also happen with really "hot" startups whose products quickly attract a cult following.

But if the right foundation isn't built at the start of the community, it can collapse just as quickly as it rises. This is why big protests flare up quickly, bringing together thousands or even millions over night, but often dissipate in a few days or weeks. They didn't have core leadership that could sustain the growth of the community. They didn't have a plan for ongoing engagement over time. They didn't create new spaces for the community to come together and engage after they took to the streets.

For established companies with lots of customers, you'll be tempted to grow your community rapidly from day one. Why not invite 10,000 customers into your new forum all at once? This would be a mistake. You'll miss out on a critical time in your community's development.

Every community starts at the seed stage. Take your time in this stage and don't worry about starting small! Small is a superpower. All big platforms start small.

Reddit started as a single page that was populated mostly by software engineers.

Facebook started on one college campus.

Twitter started as an internal communication tool for a company called Odeo.

Every religion, political party, and major city in the world once started as very small, fringe communities.

The reason starting small is so important is because of the engagement chicken-or-the-egg problem. Every community starts off with the same challenge. You need people to create content for members to engage with in the community. But you need people in the community in order to motivate people to create content.

For example, Airbnb needs people to post their rooms on the platform so that people have places to book. But people won't show up to book places until there are a lot of listings on there.

You solve this problem by shrinking down the scope of people that you're focusing on. For Airbnb, it was much easier to reach critical mass by just focusing on one city first rather than trying to fill up both sides of the marketplace everywhere in the country or the world.

For your community, it will be much easier to create social density in a smaller, more curated group. You can give every member your full attention. You can control and craft the experience intentionally. Members feel special because they feel like they're part of something new, fresh, and exclusive. You're building a strong foundation.

These early days are where your community culture is created. Sure, your culture will evolve over time, but it's much harder to make big changes to the direction once the train has left the station.

Your first members set the tone for every new member who joins after them. So you want to get the right people in there first. You want people who will be genuinely invested, and will have a high standard for the content they contribute to the community. You want givers, who are bought into creating something new together.

And you want to invest in diversity, equality, and inclusion from day one. It'll be much more difficult to inspire people from under-represented groups to join your community if you get to the growth stage and all of your members and leaders are members of the majority. Make this a priority in the seed stage and you'll have momentum as your community grows.

In the seed stage, you will spend most of your time facilitating engagement since organic engagement hasn't yet kicked in. You don't have to worry too much about scalable operations, or perfecting your measurement systems. Your priority is finding community-market fit. This phase is all about being nimble, and constantly experimenting with new engagement ideas.

In order to get members to contribute, you'll likely have to ask them directly and nudge regularly. They haven't developed a habit of coming to your community yet. There are few examples for how to participate in the community. There's no established culture, value, or trust. So you have to create it manually and find people who are comfortable with that kind of uncertainty, the early adopters.

You'll also be the only one inviting new members at first. In later stages, members will invite new members, but not in the seed stage. They have no reason to recommend the community to their friends just yet, until they participate and get value. So it's up to you to recruit.

If your community has a local leadership component where you're empowering members of your community to run their own chapters and events, then you'll likely be hosting some events yourself, and working with a few chapters to start. You're looking for the repeatable format that you can bring to chapters around the world.

Get really hands-on in this stage. As Paul Graham famously advised startups in their early days, "Do things that don't scale." Communities are just like products, or startups. In the early days you have to go above and beyond to make people happy, and focus on learning as much as possible as quickly as possible. If you have to call every single member at first to get them bought in, do that. We avoid these methods because we think, "When our community is

1000 members, there's no way I can personally call every member." But right now, you can, so you should. Do it until you can't.

The Growth Stage

If a community makes it past the seed stage, it will find itself in the growth stage.

At this stage, your community is picking up steam, you'll start to see more content and discussions organically created by the community without you having to facilitate or nudge. In online discussion-based communities, it'll move closer to 50 percent of the discussions being sparked by you, and 50 percent started by community members. And the community will start acquiring new members more organically, as existing members recommend it to others.

Your community strategy will start to become more structured. You may not have all of your measurement systems in place, or your operations streamlined, but you're on your way. You can tell a clear story and point to at least some data showing how community is impacting revenue. You might look to hire your second or third community professional on the team, as the need for specialized community roles appear. This might include a community operations manager, a programs manager, or an engagement manager.

Within your community, layers start to form as members become regulars and inner circles form. You'll start to see that distribution of activity from passive, to active, to leadership (more on that in Chapter 4).

New rules and standards will develop as you adapt in response to the good and bad experiences of the community. Communities often start with very few rules but add more as they run into situations where someone takes an action that hurts the community, but didn't technically break a rule.

You might start to see language, symbols, and other expressions of identity start to develop. Rituals will start to take shape. New roles will form in the community, informally at first, and over time become formalized, like moderator or ambassador programs.

If you're running a local leadership program then this stage is all about learning and growing. You have some ideas about the kinds of events and experiences that work well, and you're adding new insights to your playbook to help your leaders be more successful.

You're likely adding new chapters regularly, and improving your process for recruiting, approving, and onboarding new leaders.

Your job as a community builder becomes less about creation and more about facilitation. The tree is growing, and you're watering it, trimming it, keeping it healthy. You're shaping the culture, and looking for opportunities to better formalize your processes.

The Maturity Stage

At the maturity stage, the community has likely grown a good deal and now has a clear set of standards, rituals, guidelines, roles, language, symbols, and other cultural norms.

About 90 percent of the content is being created by the community at this point, and much of your job as the organizer is to manage, moderate, support leaders, and keep things running smoothly. You take on more of an operational role.

The community should have a clear set of guidelines and a system for enforcing those guidelines. There's likely a moderation team in place to be able to efficiently manage the community at scale.

For your local leadership programs, you'll now have an in-depth playbook for how to successfully run chapters and events. Team structures for local chapters will be well established, and you'll have a clear process for recruiting, approving, and onboarding new chapters. You'll have a clear system for tracking success across the entire program.

Your community strategy and operations will be well-established at this point as well. You'll likely have multiple people working on your community team, and may have multiple community teams focused on different products or parts of your business. You'll have a clear system for measuring community engagement, and business impact.

You might see a plateau in growth and engagement when the community is fully mature. It may feel less new and exciting to people. Perhaps the community became really large, and people are looking for more intimate community experiences. That's where community pollination happens.

Community Pollination

Pollination is a natural progression for communities because once it becomes too big to customize the community experience to the experience of specific groups of members, power gets redistributed.

Take for example a community for people who love music. At first, a community just for "music" might be enough to be interesting to all members. It's likely most members will be interested in a similar genre at first, let's say folk music. But the community grows and grows, it matures, and now there are tens of thousands of members with a wide range of music tastes. The people who are interested in electronic want their own space to connect. When this happens, one of two things will happen: they will form a subgroup within your community, or they will spin out their own community, outside of the spaces you've created.

Reddit is a great example of a community that handled the pollination transition really well by creating subgroups within the platform. Starting as just one page where people could share links, eventually people started posting questions on the page. There was only one page, so everything had to coexist in one feed. A lot of people weren't happy about questions being posted in the community and started complaining. It was clear that members would leave and create a new community if they couldn't find what they were looking for on Reddit.

Reddit could have made a rule that you can't post questions in the community, but that would have guaranteed those members would leave and form the community elsewhere. Instead, Reddit created the first-ever "subreddit" called "AskReddit," a separate space within the larger community, specifically dedicated to asking questions. It worked, and members loved having dedicated spaces within the larger community. Today there are over 2 million subreddits on the platform.

There are examples of communities pollinating all throughout history. Nations give birth to new nations. Religions give birth to new religions. Political factions give birth to new political factions.

In your personal life, you've likely seen friend groups merge or split out into new groups.

All groups come from existing groups.

Everything we know today as a community in society came from community members from one group deciding that their needs would be better served by creating new groups. This is core to the human experience. We can trace our community evolutions back thousands of years, and if we could find the evidence, it would go all the way back to the earliest days of human life.

As your community reaches this stage, you'll have a choice. You can fight it or you can embrace it. Fighting it will basically ensure that these members create the community elsewhere. Embracing it means distributing power to the members who step up to lead.

Those who refuse to share power will eventually lose power.

Notes

1. The 2017 Community Value and Metrics Report by CMX, December 2017, https://cmxhub.com/community-value-metrics-research.

2. "TechSmith Saves $500,000 by Crowdsourcing Snagit on Mac Development Research in Custom Get Satisfaction Community," www .businesswire.com, April 19, 2011, https://www.businesswire.com/news/ home/20110419005155/en/TechSmith-Saves-500000-Crowdsourcing-Snagit-Mac-Development.

3. "2020 Community Industry Trends Report," *CMX* (CMX, 2019), https:// cmxhub.com/community-industry-trends-report-2020.

4. "2020 Community Industry Trends Report," *CMX* (CMX, 2019), https:// cmxhub.com/community-industry-trends-report-2020.

5. Alicia Iriberri and Gondy Leroy, "A Life-Cycle Perspective on Online Community Success," *ACM Computing Surveys* 41, no. 2 (February 1, 2009): 1–29, https://doi.org/10.1145/1459352.1459356.

Chapter 3

Creating a Social Identity

So far we've discussed the business outcomes you can drive in Level 1 of your community strategy, and reviewed the specific measurable objectives that community can drive for your business.

In this chapter, we're going to move into Level 2 of your community strategy, and talk about how to build a highly engaged, healthy community.

To do this, I use a powerful tool called "the Social Identity Cycle." It explains how a member will go from being a "lurker" to becoming deeply invested in your community. Design the right social identity, and you won't be able to stop people from joining and participating in your community.

The Social Identity Cycle

At the heart of community is identity. Humans form much of our personal identities around the shared identities of the groups we participate in. We adopt the beliefs, styles, language, symbols, rituals, and other forms of expression that exist within the groups we're a part of.

When you build community, you're essentially creating a social identity. You're creating and reinforcing a set of beliefs, expressions, and actions for members to adopt and engage in. Everything you build for your community, your forums, events, logos, playbooks, etc. all exist to reinforce that shared identity and create spaces for people who share that identity to gather.

The extent to which a person adopts the shared identity will play a big role in how strongly they feel a sense of community. More than one community builder has jokingly remarked to me that they measure the success by how many members get the community logo tattooed on their body. When someone loves their community, they want the world to know it.

So a big key to building thriving communities is to develop a compelling social identity and bring anyone who shares that identity together consistently over time.

Of course, when someone first joins a community, they won't feel a strong sense of social identity within that group. They're still more of an individual in a new social space. But over time, as they participate more, and feel validated by the group, they adopt the social identity more strongly.

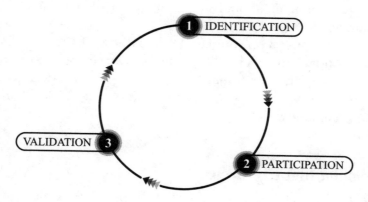

FIGURE 3.1

The Social Identity Cycle consists of three stages:
1. *Identification*. The person identifies with the community and is attracted to the social identity of the group.
2. *Participation*. The person takes some sort of action to participate in a community experience.
3. *Validation*. Participation is rewarded in some way, making them feel good about their participation, which strengthens their investment in the shared identity, and the cycle repeats.

As someone moves through the cycle over and over again, they become more invested in the community. They adopt the identity more deeply, participate in bigger and more consistent ways, and feel greater validation for their increased participation.

Over time, with consistent participation, the community member will move through three levels of identity which are laid out in the *social identity theory*[1], created in 1974 by social psychologist Henri Tajfel.

1. *Social categorization.* We see ourselves as being in the same general category as the community (e.g., I like baseball and live in New York so I'll start watching Yankees games).
2. *Social identification.* We see ourselves as a member of the group and start to adopt the shared identity (e.g., I am a Yankee fan and will wear Yankee gear to represent my fanhood).
3. *Social comparison.* We identify so strongly that we start comparing our in-group to out-groups and tie our self-esteem to the status of our group (e.g., I care deeply about the success of the Yankees, and despise the Boston Red Sox).

So you can imagine someone, going through the Social Identity Cycle over and over again, and over time, they move from categorization, to identification, to comparison.

Let's look at a real-world example of the Social Identity Cycle in action with a community called Sales Hacker. Today, Sales Hacker is the world's largest community of B2B sales professionals. When it was founded in 2013 by Max Altschuler (yup, the same guy that helped me start CMX), it was just a series of small meetups and gatherings. Max grew the community, launched conferences, and created a platform to provide sales professionals the kind of modern training and education he wished he had when first starting out.

The Sales Hacker identity sits at the core of the community's success, and it's all about the mentality that it's members embody. It's all about finding ways to work smarter and tap into new tools and technology to optimize the sales process. And it's all about being community driven. The Sales Hacker mission statement lets members know up front, "It takes a community to succeed in sales. It takes mentors, sponsors, and people who are willing to pay it forward. It takes us all, working together, helping one another."

When someone first comes to the Sales Hacker community, they're just a sales professional who's loosely interested in the Sales Hacker mentality. Over time, as they become more engaged in the community, they'll become a true "Sales Hacker," fully bought into the social identity.

So say a salesperson, let's call them Cam, hears about the Sales Hacker Community and starts going through the Social Identity Cycle:

1. **Identification.** Cam identifies as a sales professional. They find Sales Hacker when someone shares an article on Twitter that brings them to the website. They start exploring the site and find that there are thousands of sales professionals and hundreds of articles and resources just for sales professionals here. Cam's interest is piqued. They're in the "categorization" level of social identity.

2. **Participation.** The Sales Hacker content is helpful and it looks like there are a lot of good people in the community, so Cam signs up for the Sales Hacker newsletter. It's a small commitment to start, but Cam is excited to dip their toes in and learn more about the community. They also start reading a few more articles, and decide to join the Sales Hacker online community.

3. **Validation.** Cam has a great first experience with Sales Hacker. They received a really thoughtful welcome email from the team that explained the Sales Hacker mission and values which Cam felt aligned with. And Cam was personally welcomed by an admin and a bunch of members in the community. Cam feels included, and is already learning some new things from all the content. The cycle repeats …

4. **Identification.** Getting that validation made Cam feel like this is a community they could really enjoy being a part of. Cam starts to feel a stronger sense of shared identity, and specifically appreciates that this community aligns with their own values. They're still new, so they don't quite feel like they can call themselves a "Sales Hacker" just yet. But they're interested in getting more involved.

5. **Participation.** Cam takes the leap and starts participating in the community. First with just an introduction. Then they jump in on a couple threads to answer questions that other members posted. Eventually Cam posts their first discussion in the community asking a question that they're working through. Finally, Cam sees that there's an event happening in their city, and decides to attend.

6. **Validation.** Every time Cam participates, the experience has been really positive. People like Cam's comments on posts, and Cam received a lot of great answers and feedback on their discussion. Cam attended the local event and met a few really awesome people who wanted to stay in touch. They're going to get together for lunch soon. They cycle repeats again ...

7. **Identification.** It's been six months now and Cam has become a regular in the community. They proudly identify as a "Sales Hacker" and feel a strong sense of social identity. Cam's been known to wear a Sales Hacker T-shirt, and decided to put a Sales Hacker sticker they got from an event on their laptop.

8. **Participation.** Cam checks in on the community a few times a week now, has attended multiple events, and loves getting the weekly newsletter. After going to the big Sales Hacker annual conference, Cam decided they'd love to get more involved and applies to join the leadership team of their local Sales Hacker chapter. They organize events every month for local B2B sales professionals. Cam has become a big advocate for Sales Hacker and is always recommending it to other sales professionals.

9. **Validation.** Getting so involved in Sales Hacker has brought Cam a ton of value and pride. The local community is growing and Cam has developed a reputation as a strong leader in the community. Cam's gotten multiple job offers from the network, and had learned a ton throughout the whole experience. As a Sales Hacker chapter leader, Cam also gets a lot of perks like a private community, free access to events and trainings. Cam's learning a ton, growing their network, and always looking for new ways to get more involved in the community ...

... and on and on the cycle can go, as Cam feels a deepening sense of social identity, participates in greater and greater ways, and experiences lots of validation for all of their participation.

Now, of course, not all members will go through the cycle successfully. They might find that they don't align with the social identity at some point, and drop off. They might not know how to participate, or feel scared to participate, and drop off. Or they might participate, but no one responds, or they don't feel validated in any way, and so they drop off.

Drop off is normal. Your community won't be right for everyone. But there are also lots of things you can do to help members through the cycle and increase the chance that they'll become more engaged. And maybe, just maybe, a few will get a tattoo.

We'll spend the rest of this chapter on Stage 1: Identification, diving into how to create a clear and compelling social identity for your community. Then we'll get into Stage 2: Participation, in Chapters 5 and 6, and Stage 3: Validation, in Chapter 7.

Who Is Your Community Built For?

Social identities, like communities, tend to form organically over time. Remember the tree analogy for the community lifecycle? You don't have to know exactly what your community's social identity will be today. You just need to plant the seeds of community, and over time a distinct social identity will form.

That said, you should absolutely have a strong theory of who your community is built for from day one, and have a vision for the social identity you'd like to create.

On the highest level, there are three questions that will help you define the social identity of your community:

People: Who are we?

Purpose: What do we believe?

Participation: What do we do?

Answering these questions will help you better articulate the social identity to current and prospective members.

As an example for CMX:

◆ *Who are we?* We are an ambitious, empathetic, and innovative group of community professionals.
◆ *What do we believe?* That community building is the future of business, and some of the most important work in the world.
◆ *What do we do?* We gather online and offline to exchange knowledge, support each other through difficult challenges, and help each other successfully build thriving communities for our organizations.

Sometimes it's obvious, sometimes it takes some work to really hone in on who your community is, *and isn't*, for.

You may come up with a community concept, and then find that it's not compelling to anyone. The big question is, "Do people actually need this community?"

When in Doubt, Get More Specific

Generally speaking, the more specific the social identity, the more likely it will be that the people who share that identity will have a need for community.

For example, let's take a general identity, "People who ride bikes." That's a very broad identity. It's unlikely someone will see a community for "people who ride bikes" and think, "Hey, these are my people!"

So let's see if we can make the identity more specific …

People who ride *racing* bikes.

Ok … that's a little more specific. I could definitely see a community concept that's focused on gathering people who ride racing bikes. But there's a lot of room to get more specific still. People ride racing bikes for all sorts of purposes! So what if we added one of those elements to our identity?

People who ride racing bikes *and compete.*

Definitely starting to see a community opportunity here. Competitive cyclists would have a lot to talk about. But there are probably lots of communities already out there for them to choose from. So let's add a location element.

People who ride racing bikes and compete *in Austin, Texas.*

Now that's a specific identity! An Austin Competitive Cyclists community! I can imagine them having group rides and meetups and sharing awesome routes to check out. I think we're onto something here. But why stop there? Let's add some kids!

People who ride racing bikes and compete in Austin, Texas, *and are parents.*

By George, I think we have a great community in the making here. There are certainly competitive cyclists in Austin who are also parents and are working to balance their passion for cycling with spending time with their family. Perhaps they can organize family rides and coordinate on the range of specific challenges that they all share.

All of these are social identities. All of these can be considered "communities." But you can see how as the identity gets more specific, the people who share that identity are more likely to have a lot of the same goals and challenges in common, and have more opportunities to help each other. The identity is more meaningful. It'll be easier to create a community and a strong sense of belonging for those people.

If I'm a software engineer, and I'm already a part of an engineering community that I love, I don't have a need for another community. It'll be difficult to get me to participate in a new community for engineers.

If I'm an engineer in a city where there aren't many engineers, or if I just haven't found a community where I feel like I truly belong, then I'll be actively or passively seeking community.

Occasionally, the opportunity can be found by making the identity more broad as well. A great example is a community founded by Allison Esposito Medina. While working at Google in 2015 she, like most women in tech, faced a lot of challenges that come with working in a male-dominated industry. But most of the communities for women working in technology were centered around female engineers, a very specific identity. Allison worked in tech, but was a content manager, not an engineer. She felt like there needed to be a community for all women who worked in tech. Tech Ladies was born! The community has grown to over 100,000 members, providing them with a safe space to support and celebrate each other, and has helped hundreds of women land jobs in tech. Turns out, there were a lot of women in tech who were looking for community.

Look for the People Who Feel Isolated

When we feel isolated, we start looking for community. It's human nature. When we see a group of people that we identify with, we're drawn to it. Communities are like centers of gravity in that way, a burning sun drawing the isolated and lonely into its warm embrace.

People may seem well connected but have some part of their identity where they feel isolated. They might feel connected with friends and family but isolated in their work. They might feel connected to their colleagues, but might be looking for colleagues who share their same race or sexual orientation. That competitive cyclist in Austin might have a great support network, but they felt like they were the only one who was a parent AND rode competitively.

There's a good chance that everyone has some part of their identity where they feel lonely. There's always an opportunity for community. You just need to find the isolated identity.

I often hear people say, "There are already so many communities focused on fill-in-the-blank, do we really need another one?"

Just because there's already a community focused on your broader topic, that doesn't mean you can't still create a valuable community for people. Who does your audience want to connect with, but can't? What do they want to be able to share, but they don't have a safe space to do so? What part of their identity do they need a space to express?

If you can give someone a safe space to express themselves and get value in a way they can't anywhere else, a thriving community awaits.

Who Doesn't Belong?

A helpful exercise for defining who your ideal member is to ask yourself, "Who doesn't belong?"

That doesn't mean your community won't be inclusive. Every community has people who belong and people who don't belong. Even if your community is open for anyone to join some people will feel like they align with your values and practices, and some won't.

That's a good thing.

Every community can't serve everyone. Being focused lets you create welcoming, safe spaces for specific groups of people who don't have one in their existing communities.

Inclusivity does not mean including everyone on earth. All communities are exclusive in some way.

Communities are groups of people with a common interest, a common belief, a common set of values ... which means there will be people who share that commonality, and people who don't.

Don't feel guilty when excluding people, because it's the exclusion that makes members feel safe, knowing that the people in the room are those they can trust, and whose values they align with.

The Young Entrepreneur Council is a great example. It's a community that requires that all members have either raised over $1 million, or generate over $1 million in revenue. This lets all the members in the community know that if someone is a member, they aren't a beginner and they probably have similar challenges with growing their business. They know that there will be a certain level of experience and specificity of conversation because of that exclusivity.

Ethel's Club is another great example. Ethel's Club started as a coworking space designed for people of color, and evolved into a full social and wellness club with both offline and online spaces. As Ethel's Club's Founder Naj Austin once told me, "When a community makes someone feel seen for who they are, everything else just kind of falls into place." As soon as her members walk in the door, they see books published by black authors, art created by black creatives, and lots of mirrors so they can see *themselves* in the space. These little things make all the difference, and within months of launching members would tell Naj that Ethel's Club has completely changed their life by making them feel seen and accepted in the professional world for the first time. White people are of course welcome in the space, but it's not designed intentionally for them the way most of society is.

One more great example can be found with The Dinner Party, a potluck dinner community that's hosted in over 150 cities around the world. It's specifically for people in their twenties to forties who experienced the loss of a loved one. The founders Carla Fernandez and Lennon Flowers created this space because the support groups they found were mostly comprised of folks from older generations. They wanted to connect with people their own age to support each other and process their grief. By creating a space dedicated to their own age group, they could talk about challenges that are impacting them specifically, that older generations aren't experiencing. Does that exclude someone in their sixties who might want to participate in this experience? Yes. But it's important to draw the line, to make sure your members know that this is a safe space for them. A space designed *specifically* for them.

Keep in mind that one of the worst feelings in the world for humans is to feel excluded. Especially if it's a group that they believe they should belong to. Exclude with empathy. Exclude with the knowledge that not everyone has a community to turn to, and while yours might not be perfect for them, it might be the closest thing they can find.

It's good to be exclusive, as long as it's intentional and moral.

If you're concerned about excluding people unfairly, ask yourself, "Whose voices aren't present in the room that *should* be?"

If you find that there are people not represented that should be in your community, that's your red flag.

Inclusivity, when done right, ensures that the right voices are in the room, and that there aren't biases, and inequalities, preventing voices from being in the room that *should* be in the room.

Otherwise, embrace exclusivity to the extent that it gives members a community that's compelling, and safe.

Investing in Diversity, Equity, and Inclusion from Day One

While it's important to exclude the wrong people, it's even more important that you're not excluding the right people.

I'm not an expert on diversity, equity, and inclusion (DEI), and I can't claim to have made it a priority when we started CMX. I'm a white cis male who just wasn't very aware of my privilege and the level of intention it would require to counterbalance the conscious and unconscious bias that exists in society. But it's something we've made into a nonnegotiable priority over the last few years, bringing in out-side experts to educate our team and community members, improving our policies and processes, prioritizing putting people from underrepresented groups on our stage and in leadership positions.

One important lesson I've learned is that DEI is inseparable from community building. As soon as you make the choice to create a social identity, you start making choices about who belongs and who doesn't. You can either perpetuate the norms, and miss out on the incredible value of having diverse voices in your community, or you can make it an intention and take action.

We live in a society that does not treat people equally. People are oppressed, exploited, and treated as "lesser than" in everything from job opportunities, to the justice system, to the quality of medical treatment all because of the color of their skin, ethnicity, gender, religion, or sexual orientation.

When you build a community, you get to choose what's considered "normal." You can create spaces that feel wholly different from the rest of society, and make people feel like they're welcome and belong, regardless of their background.

Being passive isn't going to bring about change. Without taking action, your community will perpetuate these norms. It's the world we live in, and it's very easy to maintain the status quo. It's much harder to make your community an agent of change.

With intention, communities are one of the most powerful tools we have for fighting systemic racism, sexism and other forms of social discrimination and exploitation that exists in society today.

A big part of creating change will be driven by who you put in positions of power. Whether it's a moderator, a council member, an ambassador, or any other position of authority, make sure that you are seeking out and promoting folks from underrepresented groups to put in those positions.

When you host events for your community, make sure to actively seek out speakers, experts, and mentors from underrepresented groups. We aim to reach 40 percent representation of underrepresented groups on our conference stage every year. Review your designs and communications to ensure the language and imagery are authentically inclusive of the groups that you want to feel welcome in your community.

It's not enough to just open up opportunities for people. If they're underrepresented, there are a lot of roadblocks preventing them from accessing your community and leadership positions. They may not hear about the opportunities in the first place because they don't have access to the same networks. They might not see people who look like them in your community, and assume they won't be included.

They may also consider themselves unqualified for a position. For example, studies show that men apply for a job when they meet only 60 percent of the qualifications, but women apply only if they meet 100 percent of them.[2] So you have to proactively seek out under-represented voices, invite them into leadership positions, and do the work to make sure that they're set up for success if they choose to take on the role.

That's why it's important you don't wait to make DEI a priority. As Naj Austin from Ethel's Club explains, "It's extremely difficult to change the culture of a community once it's already established. You have to start from day one."

The initial group that joins a community is often highly influenced by the personal network of the founder, and founding members. That means there's a good chance that without intention, the community will be lacking in diversity. Over time the similar identities in the community will be reinforced, and as it grows it will be more and more difficult to attract diverse members. They'll look around, not see anyone who looks like them, and question whether they'll feel included in your space.

It's the same for starting a company. Say all the founders and founding team are white and mostly male. When its 10 people on the team, that may not feel too unreasonable. The team may think, "It's super early days; this thing might not even work. We can always invest in diversity later."

Then, things pick up speed and the company starts growing. The next 10 people end up looking a lot like the first 10, since everyone came through references by current staff. Soon there are 50 employees and the staff is looking extra white and male.

Now, it's going to be a lot more difficult to hire someone of color, because they're going to take one look around and see that they don't belong there. And you'll lose the opportunity to bring in important, diverse voices and backgrounds to contribute to your community. Your community will look more and more uniform.

Before you scale your community, put into place values, guidelines, and operations you want to bring to the world. Make DEI a core value from the start. Do it in the early days, before it feels like a problem. By creating these standards early, you'll give your community a shot at having a healthy balance in the future.

Wherever you're starting from today, just start. As Ibram X. Kendi reminds us in his book *How to Be an Antiracist*,[3] "Like fighting an addiction," "being an antiracist requires persistent self-awareness, constant self-criticism, and regular self-examination." Building more inclusive communities and actively fighting racism is something you'll be working on for as long as you're building communities. You won't have all the answers on day one, and maybe not ever. But you have to just start trying.

We have a long way to go at CMX since we didn't make it a priority from day one, and we probably will never have a truly diverse, equitable, and inclusive community as a result. But we've made the commitment to improving every day. We've seen the impact that this work has had on helping our team and community become more diverse and inclusive. I know for certain that the next community I start won't miss the opportunity to be an agent for change.

What Is Your Community's Personality?

When brainstorming social identities, I like to think about community identity as if it's a person. Like a person, a community will have a personality and the right people will feel drawn to that personality.

A community with a personality I felt very drawn to when it first launched was Product Hunt. There were hundreds of communities for startups and entrepreneurs when Ryan Hoover decided to build Product Hunt, a community where members could submit new products they discovered, and others could vote and comment on those products, with a new list starting every day.

What made Product Hunt so successful wasn't so much the topic he was focusing on or the platform itself. It was the unique voice Ryan brought to the startup world. Other communities, like Hacker News, were known for being overly critical and negative in its judgments of new startups. Founders would dread the comment section if their startups were ever listed. Ryan, on the other hand, was known for being humble, kind, and unapologetically supportive of all product ideas, regardless of how simple or silly they seemed. His personality translated to the culture, and personality, of the Product Hunt community.

On Product Hunt, the tone was always positive. It attracted founding members who vibed with the more positive culture, and who were also intrinsically kind and supportive. Members were encouraged to be supportive of all products in the community (assuming it didn't violate the community guidelines), and unnecessary negativity was actively addressed and moderated. Critical feedback was always welcome, of course – but always with the intention of helping the creators out, not putting them down.

Similarly, when we started CMX, we wanted to create a distinct voice from the other communities for community professionals out there. We intentionally avoided using jargon, instead using simple, accessible language. Where a lot of people used a negative tone when talking about the opportunity to work in community management, we wanted to make CMX a positive, highly energized space. We wanted our community to feel relatable, down-to-earth, and fun. That personality shows up in everything from the copy on our website, to the design of our events, to how we welcome members into the community.

Every community has its own personality. It's the personality of your community that can truly set it apart from the alternatives. A community can be professional, playful, hungry, empathetic, inspired, laid-back, quirky, funny – anything you could identify in a person, you can identify in a group of people. Are all the existing communities too uptight for your taste? Start a community that's more laid-back and informal.

Keep in mind the personality of the community will often mimic the personality of its leaders, since they set the example, and draw in people who align with their personality in the early days of the community, like Ryan did. So choose your leaders wisely.

How Can You Make Your Members Feel "Cool"?

Like many kids, I spent most of my childhood trying to fit in with the cool kids (and failing miserably).

We like to think that we stop caring about being cool as we get older, but the truth is we care just as much, we just redefine what we view as "cool."

In American middle and high schools, we live in a social bubble, and what's "cool" is generally pretty clear: good looking, wealthy, athletic, care-free, popular. As we get older and expand our social networks, we reframe our concept of cool. We find acceptance around different kinds of hobbies, passions, and identities. Ultimately, that's what being cool is: being accepted by a group of people that you care about. And we realize we can find acceptance by being weird, creating art, listening to rebellious music, reading books … any topic that others are also interested in.

To build a successful community, you want to be perceived as "cool" to the people who care about that topic. If you want to start a community for your customers, you have to make a space that your customers will aspire to be a part of because it will make them feel cool to be a member.

There are a lot of industries that are considered "unsexy" out there. Whenever I see an unsexy industry, I know there's an opportunity to build a great community. Take software testers as an example. Not the most exciting professional community out there … that is, until the Ministry of Testing community showed up. It's founder, Rosie Sherry, was a software tester herself, and found that all the existing communities and conferences for software testers were really boring and overpriced. She wished there was a community that was more fun, and accessible, for software testers to join. The Ministry of Testing was born. She designed the community to be fun and playful. All over their website and events you'll find colorful cartoon monsters that serve as sort of mascots for the community. It doesn't feel boring at all. It's a community that makes software testers feel cool.

"Being cool" is really about being accepted for who you are.

In the *sense of community theory*, and most definitions of community, emotional safety is a critical element. The true power of community is to help people become more authentic versions of themselves.

"Just be yourself" is common advice today. But we understand ourselves best through the communities we participate in. It's the feedback we get from the people around us that shapes what we feel comfortable putting out there into the world, and what we keep locked up, hidden from the world, and often hidden from ourselves.

By creating a community where someone can express a part of themselves safely, in a way they can't express that part of themselves anywhere else, you empower them to discover who they truly are.

For generations, the LGBTQ community had to live in hiding. In some parts of the world, they still do. San Francisco became a safe home for LGBTQ people to come out because there was a community that accepted and celebrated them. They could express themselves fully. There was still fear of being attacked, but there was enough of an established community that they could feel empowered taking that risk, knowing they weren't alone.

Sherry's story of starting the Ministry of Testing reminded me of my own story with CMX. 10 years ago, there were few people who would have called community management cool. I mean … I thought it was cool. But I couldn't find a group that aligned with how I saw the space. Community managers were misunderstood, undervalued, paid poorly, lacked role models, and so we felt anything but cool. We all felt like we were trying to figure out who we were in the world of business.

We started CMX Summit with the intention of creating a space that would make community professionals into the hero. For 355 days out of the year, they might feel misunderstood, but on that one day, at our event, they'd feel like rock stars. We celebrated them, told them how important their work was and would become, and put role models on stage.

We were specific about the language we used. Instead of "community managers," which has a connotation of a low-level position, we referred to them as "community professionals." Instead of "community management," we'd say "the community industry." We didn't start a "blog" with "posts," we had a "publication" with "articles." This was all to communicate legitimacy and importance. We wanted community professionals to feel valued and proud. We wanted to make community management cool.

Five years later, we're hosting conferences with thousands of community professionals gathering for multiple days. We're putting CEOs of multibillion-dollar companies, and world-leading experts on stage, who align with our message of the importance and value of community. At CMX, community professionals are the coolest people in the world.

And that's the power of community. You create a safe space for a group of people to be proud of who they are, and they will pass on that safety, that celebration, to the next group of people struggling to express themselves. Slowly, over time, community changes the world, by changing how people express themselves.

Should Your Community Have a Unique Identity from Your Company Brand?

Another big question for companies thinking about their community identity is whether they should build community around their existing brand and product identity or create a unique brand identity just for their community.

There are lots of great examples of companies who decided to give their community its own unique brand and identity.

Culture Amp created the "People Geek" brand for their community of HR and People Ops professionals. Its conference "Culture First" became another community brand that they eventually adopted.

The mobile analytics platform Branch Metrics hosts regular events and experiences for their customers in what they call "The Mobile Growth Community," opting to adopt the identity of the category they're hoping to own.

Honeybook is a small business software company that acquired the Rising Tide Society, a community for small businesses, just two weeks after the community launched. It saw the opportunity to invest in a great community brand and founder in Natalie Franke and it's paid huge dividends for them. Rising Tide Society is now a thriving community of over 50,000 small businesses and 475 local chapters.

That community has set up Honeybook as a community leader, and drives significant annual recurring revenue.

Hubspot is a great example of a company that intentionally built a community brand around the category they wanted to own. The "Inbound" community has become a well-known brand in the marketing world, which consists of online spaces and in person conferences and events for inbound marketers. They wanted to own the topic of *inbound marketing* in people's minds. So they branded the community around the category rather than calling it the "Hubspot community." Now it's hard to think of inbound marketing without thinking of Hubspot.

A good rule of thumb is that if you have product–market fit, you can build a community around your product. But if people don't care about your product yet, then they're not going to care enough to participate in a community focused on it. So it might be better to focus your community on the broader market or category in order to start building your community and audience. If you successfully build a healthy community for your target market, you'll be perceived as a leader and earn a great deal of trust.

Once you have loyal customers, then it definitely makes sense to build spaces just for customers as well. Customers will be a unique identity, with much more specific needs than the broader category. So you can dedicate spaces where they can share best practices around using your product, give their feedback, and support each other.

Ultimately, you can always do both. It really depends on your goals. If you're focused on growing your market and market share, then build a community for the broader category that you're working in. If your goals are more focused on retention and customer success, then start off with a focus on your customers. Salesforce has a massive Salesforce branded community program focused on customer support, and then created the "Trailblazer" community as a unique social identity for their customers focused on learning and career growth.

You can also keep your company brand but host more interest-based discussions that don't have to do with your product. For example, collaboration software giant Atlassian has both customer support forums, and interest-based groups, all living in their single online community space. It's all branded as the "Atlassian community," so they chose not to create a unique brand for their community. That means it's less likely that people will participate there if they're not a customer. But it gives their customers much more to talk about than just the product.

I'm a big fan of building a community with its own unique brand. It's how we work at Bevy and CMX. CMX started independently, of course, and was acquired by Bevy about five years later. But we never let that affect the trust and objectivity of the CMX community. It's that trust that brings the most value to Bevy. Every time a salesperson talks to a prospect, they can offer CMX training or events to help that prospect learn and grow. The majority of the time, they find that the prospect is already a member of the CMX community, and so there's a lot of established trust. CMX has driven millions in pipeline for Bevy because when someone participates in the community, they organically and authentically start to learn about Bevy, too. And since Bevy is a community and events software platform, we use it for all CMX events, which means all of our members get to experience the product firsthand.

Now, building a community for your broader industry doesn't come without its challenges. A community that's designed and branded for the industry will only thrive if it's authentic and objective. That means you might end up having competitors in the community, and that has to be okay. If you don't allow competitors in your space, then you can't truly claim to be the industry's community, can you? You might be publishing content under the community brand and feel tempted to promote your own software product. But those kinds of direct promotions will just communicate to your members that your priority is not them, it's selling your software.

I'm a big believer that you most always have a "Community First" value. If you want to be *the* community where your industry gathers, then you have to stay authentic and objective. Communities are really good at smelling a sales pitch from a mile away.

Finding Sub-Identities within Your Community

Even after you've homed in on an identity for your community, it's likely that you'll find sub-identities within your community, especially if it's a large, mature audience.

For example, when working with the Google team on their G2G program, we found that a key challenge was the sheer size of Google and range of employees who worked there. A G2G member could be anyone from a salesperson to a fitness coach to an engineer. Each group had unique learning needs and goals. So in order to build an engaging community program, they needed to break down their larger identity (Google employees) into their sub-identities (e.g., sales, fitness, engineering).

By looking at each group individually, we were able to consider how the community could serve them more specifically. And we designed different social identities that would resonate with each group.

Your community could be "all of our customers," but you should think about the different kinds of customers or members you have, and how a community might serve them differently.

There are all kinds of criteria you can use to break down your overall community identity into sub-identities:

- ◆ *Contribution level.* Focus on your most active users, or most loyal customers (e.g., eBay PowerSellers, Airbnb Superhosts).
- ◆ *Industry.* Focus on your biggest markets, or the industries where members have the biggest need for community (e.g., Google for Education, Hubspot's Inbound Conference).
- ◆ *Location.* Focus on members who live in specific regions where you have critical mass (e.g., Google Developer Groups, Twitch Meetups).
- ◆ *Demographics.* Focus on members with common age, gender, race, or other attributes (e.g., Black Girls Code, Tech Ladies, Ethel's Club).

A simple exercise you can use to explore the identities in your community is creating an identity tree like the one in Figure 3.2.

Put the overarching identity of your community at the top. Then in each level, you can break down the identity into its subgroups based on any criteria. For example, in Google's G2G program we could break down the overarching identity (G2G instructors) into the different kinds of professions they represent (see Figure 3.3).

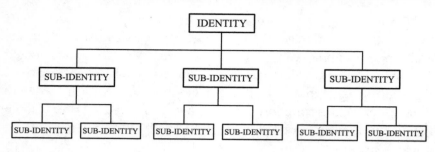

Figure 3.2

Figure 3.3

As you get more specific, you can already start to imagine how the community engagement plan will differ for each group.

Defining Identity by Levels of Contribution

Within every mature community, you'll also find that there are many layers of social identity based on the type, or level of contribution.

As you can see in Figure 3.4, you can visualize it like a solar system with different levels of social gravity pulling members toward the middle. At the center, the level of commitment is strongest and relationships are most dense, making gravity at the center stronger than in the outer rings.

You have your most loyal, most committed members (leaders) at the center. Then you have your power members, active members, passive members, and so on.

As you move toward the innermost rings, the shared identity is more meaningful to the member, and they're more likely to feel a

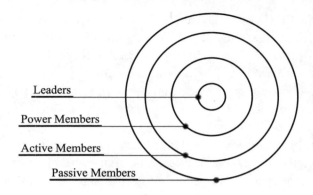

Leaders

Power Members

Active Members

Passive Members

FIGURE 3.4

stronger sense of belonging. As you move outward, the shared identity becomes less meaningful, and the sense of belonging is weaker.

The titles of *leaders, power, active,* and *passive* are general buckets that you may use to understand the different kinds of participation in your community. But you might find that your community has more specific names or roles for the different levels of identity within your community.

Let's look at Airbnb as an example. Consider all the levels of social identity that exists under the "Airbnb" umbrella identity:

1. I'm aware of Airbnb.
2. I'm registered on Airbnb.
3. I'm a guest on Airbnb.
4. I'm a host on Airbnb.
5. I'm a "Super Host" on Airbnb.
6. I work at Airbnb.
7. I cofounded Airbnb.

All of these identities are part of the "Airbnb community." Identities 5–7 are likely to feel a stronger sense of belonging and commitment deep enough to make it a meaningful community in their lives. Identities 3 and 4 probably feel the community magic a little bit. Identities 1 and 2, not so much.

It's OK that identities 1 and 2 don't find it meaningful. You don't need them to. They're part of the outer rings of this ecosystem.

They're the "audience" or the "consumer," which is critical to the ecosystem, because the hosts and the Airbnb team won't be motivated to contribute if there isn't an audience there to consume.

You will always have leaders at the center who are creating and facilitating community, power members who are your top contributors, active members who participate regularly, and passive members who mostly just consume.

As you break down your community into the different types and levels of contribution, you'll likely find that there are different identities, and needs for community. When designing your community engagement strategy, get clear on which identities you're focusing on.

Notes

1. H. Tajfel, "Social Identity and Intergroup Behaviour," *Social Science Information* 13 (2) (April 1, 1974): 65–93, https://doi.org/10.1177/053901847401300204.

2. Tara Sophia Mohr, "Why Women Don't Apply for Jobs Unless They're 100% Qualified," *Harvard Business Review* (March 2, 2018), https://hbr.org/2014/08/why-women-dont-apply-for-jobs-unless-theyre-100-qualified.

3. Ibram X. Kendi, *How to Be an Antiracist*, One World; First Edition (August 13, 2019) (Vintage, 2020).

Chapter 4

Mapping the Community Participation Journey

N ow that you have the first stage in the Social Identity Cycle under your belt, we're ready to move into the second stage, participation.

The participation stage is all about understanding the journey that a member goes through in your community over time, and facilitating spaces and experiences that move them along that journey. Early in the journey, it's likely that members will participate in smaller and more passive ways. Over time, as they move through the cycle, they'll become more committed and participate in greater ways, taking on larger roles in the community. In this chapter, you'll learn how to design your community member journey and give your members a range of opportunities to contribute.

We'll talk about how to attract and onboard new members, how to create a "power user" status, and what you need to do to activate community leaders who will contribute to facilitating engagement in your community.

The Commitment Curve

When we think about community participation, we tend to just think about the big actions we want community members to take, like posting in a forum, attending an event, organizing events, and becoming power users or leaders.

In truth, there are going to be a whole lot of actions, small and large, that someone can take along their journey of becoming an engaged member of your community. Participation can be as simple as reading a blog post or subscribing to a newsletter to start. Then as someone moves through the Social Identity Cycle over and over again, and they become more invested in the community, they will be more likely to participate in greater ways.

It's your job as the community builder to facilitate that experience for your members. You want to understand all the different ways that someone can participate in your community and, using the cycle, move them along that journey.

A useful tool for mapping out this journey is called the *commitment curve*. The concept of a commitment curve was first developed by Darrel Conner and Robert Pattison in 1982 as a tool to explain how an individual adopts organizational change over time.[1] The commitment curve was later adapted to communities for the purpose of understanding how an individual becomes more committed and takes greater actions within a community over time.

I first learned about the commitment curve from Douglas Atkin when he was the chief community officer for Meetup back in 2008. The goal at Meetup was clear: get more people to host meetups. Millions of people had signed up for Meetup, but if there weren't events for them to go to, they wouldn't stay engaged and the platform would plateau.

When Atkin dug into the experience that members were having and researched why they weren't starting their own events, the answer became clear. Meetup was asking its members to host events, which is a huge commitment to the community, right when they signed up. They weren't committed enough to participate in that big way, and so they would just drop off and not participate at all.

"Welcome to our community; please make a massive commitment of time and energy!" isn't a very logical way to motivate people to do something, but that's exactly how a lot of communities and community products are designed. We, as the organizers, know what we want our members to do, but we're impatient and want them to jump right to the high-commitment contributions. For the majority of our members, it will take time for them to get to the point where they're committed enough to participate at that level. You need to make smaller asks first.

This is where the commitment curve comes in. The idea is that over time, your members' level of commitment will increase. As their commitment to the community increases, their willingness to make larger and larger contributions to the community goes up. So you need to only make smaller asks of members at the beginning of the curve, and increase the ask as they move up the curve.

Figure 4.1 shows what Atkin's commitment curve looked like at Meetup.

Instead of welcoming members to the community and immediately asking them to host a meetup, they started easing members into the community with smaller asks. *Fill out your profile. Add a picture. Read a blog. Subscribe. And when you're ready, maybe attend a Meetup so you can get a feel for the community.*

Now, all members aren't going to follow the commitment curve exactly the way you draw it up. Some members will join and find the community to be such a good fit that they're ready to take action and make larger contributions right away. Some members might spend years in your community and never quite get to the point where they feel motivated to increase their commitment. And some members will move up the curve, and back down the curve as their life and needs change, or the community changes.

By mapping out your community commitment curve, you can lay out all the different actions you want your community members to take, and make sure you're asking for bigger commitments only when members are ready to make that commitment.

The Four Levels of Participation

Remember that once your community reaches the late growth and maturity stages of the community lifecycle, you'll find that a natural striation of participation levels start to form. In Chapter 3, we talked about how communities will form different buckets of participation as *passive members, active members, power members,* and *leaders.*

We can map these levels to the commitment curve to better understand the phases that a member goes through as they become a more committed member of your community. Figure 4.2 shows how you could break down Atkin's Meetup Commitment Curve, for example.

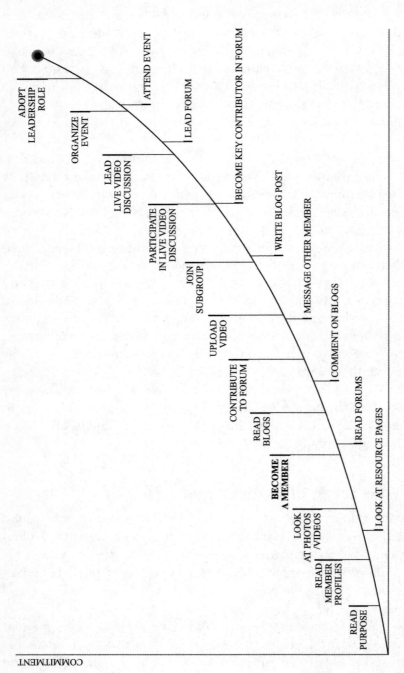

COMMITMENT

ADOPT
LEADERSHIP
ROLE

ORGANIZE
EVENT

ATTEND EVENT

LEAD
LIVE VIDEO
DISCUSSION

LEAD FORUM

BECOME KEY CONTRIBUTOR IN FORUM

PARTICIPATE
IN LIVE VIDEO
DISCUSSION

JOIN
SUBGROUP

WRITE BLOG POST

UPLOAD
VIDEO

MESSAGE OTHER MEMBER

CONTRIBUTE
TO FORUM

COMMENT ON BLOGS

READ
BLOGS

**BECOME
A MEMBER**

READ FORUMS

LOOK
AT PHOTOS
/VIDEOS

LOOK AT RESOURCE PAGES

READ
MEMBER
PROFILES

READ
PURPOSE

FIGURE 4.1

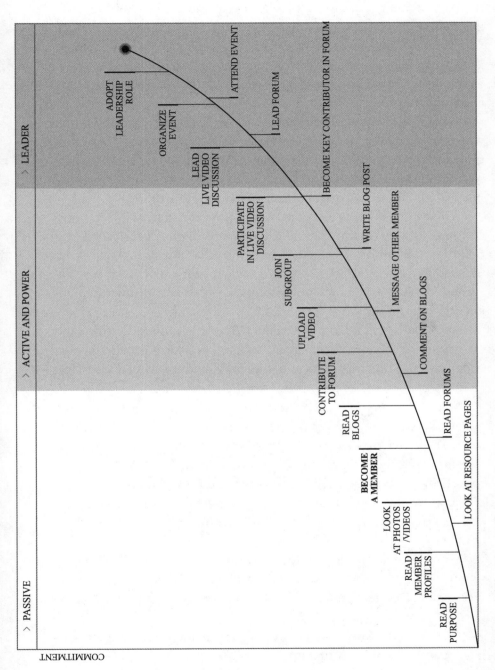

COMMITMENT

> PASSIVE   > ACTIVE AND POWER   > LEADER

READ PURPOSE
READ MEMBER PROFILES
LOOK AT PHOTOS /VIDEOS
BECOME A MEMBER
READ BLOGS
CONTRIBUTE TO FORUM
UPLOAD VIDEO
JOIN SUBGROUP
PARTICIPATE IN LIVE VIDEO DISCUSSION
LIVE VIDEO DISCUSSION
ORGANIZE EVENT
ADOPT LEADERSHIP ROLE

LOOK AT RESOURCE PAGES
READ FORUMS
COMMENT ON BLOGS
MESSAGE OTHER MEMBER
WRITE BLOG POST
BECOME KEY CONTRIBUTOR IN FORUM
LEAD FORUM
ATTEND EVENT

FIGURE 4.2

83

Passive members are folks who are at the start of the commitment curve. They're participating in smaller, lower-commitment ways, mostly consuming content, learning, and listening. A passive member is what we often call an audience member, or lurker. They don't contribute by creating any content or engaging in any discussion, they just want to listen for now.

An active member is someone who participates by joining in the discussion and creating content. They're a bit further up the commitment curve. In digital spaces, they're creating new discussions or responding to existing discussions. In physical spaces they're meeting people, joining in discussions, and sharing their learnings.

A power member is someone who is so committed to the community, so engaged, that they contribute at very high rates. They're the first one to jump on a lot of new threads in your forum. They show up to every event. They use your product religiously. Like we discussed in Chapter 4, sometimes companies create a distinct identity just for their power users.

And finally you'll have the leaders. These are the folks who take on roles like moderating a digital space, becoming an admin of a subgroup, or launching a local community chapter. They create and facilitate spaces and experiences for other members.

Now it's common logic to say, "Great! Now in order to build an engaged community we just need to motivate all of our passive members to be active or power members!" But the truth is that ALL of these roles are critical to communities. Passive members play an important role. They provide the eyes and ears that the active and power members care about. Without the passive members there to consume, the active and power members have less of an audience to consume their content.

You'll ultimately need all four levels for a large, mature community to work: leaders, a core group of power members, a consistent group of active members, and an often-larger group of passive members.

An engaged community is an ecosystem made up of people moving up and down the commitment curve over time.

And every individual member's journey will be different. Members can, and often will, skip around up and down the curve. They might jump ahead to be an active member right away. I've seen people join the CMX community and feel so inspired that they immediately apply to start a local chapter. Members can also fall back down the curve if they fall out of the Social Identity Cycle and no longer identify with the group, no longer feel motivated to participate, or no longer feel validated for their participation.

So the idea that all members need a lot of time to become a committed member of your community isn't always true. Sometimes when they're the right fit, they can go from zero to 60 real fast.

Generally, you want to focus your engagement strategy on the inner circles. The Pareto principle applies here, which predicts that roughly 80 percent of the content in your community will be created by 20 percent of your members. While this principle doesn't apply to all communities, it's a common distribution found in large social platforms. So you want to make sure that 20 percent is set up to be really happy, engaged, and successful. You'll grow your community a lot faster by working to get that 20 percent to double their commitment than by trying to get the other 80 percent of your community to increase their commitment by fivefold.

But remember that all the layers are important. YouTube has many, many layers of identities in their ecosystem. Of course, it's the creators on YouTube, the people posting videos consistently, that create the value on the platform. But without the 99.9 percent of users who just watch videos there to consume, those creators don't have a reason to create, so it's all needed to make the ecosystem work. YouTube spends a lot of energy building tools to make it easier for users to consume content and subscribe to creators. Lyft drivers won't participate if there aren't people to book rides. eBay sellers won't post their items for sale if there isn't anyone there to buy. The creators need the consumers.

Prioritize keeping your inner rings engaged and successful. But don't forget about the outer rings and the value of your audience. Make it easy for your passive consumers to passively consume. Get them the content they need in the most efficient way possible. Love your lurkers.

How to Attract Members to Your Community

If you look at any complete commitment curve, you'll find that the member journey starts before they officially become a member. They'll have to hear about your community first, do their research, and make a decision to join.

How people find your community will depend on the stage of your community, the kind of community you're building, and how established your existing audience is.

If your community is still in the seed stage, I recommend starting with a minimum viable community (MVC). The idea is that you don't need a big, automated community program to validate that people actually need your community and are interested in the social identity you're gathering. You can build a very simple, manually powered version of your community and start getting member feedback much more quickly.

You should plan on no organic growth in the early days.

There's this rosy picture that people like to paint when talking about community building. A person has an idea for a community, hosts their first event, and it catches like wildfire! It grows and grows until wow, it's a global community!

This narrative is misleading. It makes us think that if we can just set up the right circumstances – the right message, in the right space, with the right programming – then people will flock to our communities. It's that "if you build it they will come" energy.

They won't come. If a community grows organically from day one, it is the extreme exception to the rule. In reality, every community builder I've ever spoken to talks about how hard they had to work to get their first members in the door. Most communities start small and stay small, never expanding beyond the first group of founding members. The ones that get big are a direct result of leaders working to recruit new members, spread awareness, and essentially market their community like you would any other product or service.

Of course, organic growth sounds a lot better from a marketing perspective. There's a temptation to make it look like we didn't have to work very hard for our community growth. We want it to look like our community was so awesome, it just grew on its own. A lot of businesses brag about spending $0 on marketing for the same reason.

Behind the scenes, you'll find a team hustling, sending emails, hosting events, promoting content, and doing everything they can to fill their funnel.

Hope for organic growth, but plan for manual growth. Get ready to roll up your sleeves and *make* it grow. Any organic, "word-of-mouth" growth that you get on top is gravy. Just don't rely on it.

When we first decided to host CMX Summit, before we even had a website, I sent around 300 personal emails to people asking them if they'd be interested in a conference for community professionals. If they said yes, I'd personally follow up with the ticket page once it was up and say, "Great! Here you go. See you there!"

When Ryan Hoover built the Product Hunt community, the first members were sourced from a series of brunch events he was hosting for entrepreneurs and product lovers. I was one of them! After months of hosting events, he emailed all of us and asked what we thought of a new idea he had where people could share cool products they discovered. Product Hunt was born! The first iteration was a group of less than 100 of us just sending Ryan our favorite products over email, and he would put them into a newsletter that people could subscribe to. It was a huge hit, and it start growing quickly. But it was only because Ryan took the time to build the foundation of community with a small group first. That group created the foundation of community, and a center of gravity that others were drawn to.

Both CMX and Product Hunt were very hands-on and personal in the early days. Look at any large community today and it's almost guaranteed that the founders were personally inviting members in the early days. Sarah Leary, cofounder and former CEO of NextDoor, talks about how in the very early days, they were literally knocking on people's doors to invite them to join the platform and try to get a critical mass of members for that neighborhood.

It will be easier to get your community off the ground if you already have an established audience and a foundation of trust. For example, if you already have 1,000 customers who use and love your product, it'll be easier to launch a forum and motivate people to become members – though I'd still recommend starting small, and with personal outreach. Being hands-on will make those first members feel special, and make them value the community more than if they just receive an invitation in a mass email.

Once you have the foundation of community, and you start finding community-market fit, your community will move into the growth state of the lifecycle and people will start to come to your community more organically. Members will invite other members rather than you having to invite everyone yourself. You can facilitate this experience by giving your members a certain number of invites each. Product Hunt did this in its early days, giving each of the founding members three invites. Because the community was so high quality, and the invites were limited, members took them seriously and only invited members that they thought would be valuable additions to the community. In the late growth and maturity stages, word of mouth often becomes the biggest driver of growth. Most people find out about CMX today because they bring up a challenge they're thinking about related to community, and another member recommends they check out our community.

Once your community is growing or mature, it's okay to take more of an automated, or traditional marketing approach, to growing your community. You should make sure your community is listed clearly on your website. If it's a customer community, think about where your community can show up on different parts of your website where your customers are already spending time, like in dashboards or in help documents. At CMX, we're constantly publishing articles and research to grow our audience, and then inviting that audience to join our community spaces through our newsletter and links from our website.

The platform you choose to host your community on can also be a driver of community growth. If you host your community on Facebook, Slack, Reddit, LinkedIn, or any large social network, you can tap into their network effects and recommendation engines. A lot of people find CMX through our Facebook group, which gets recommended to users who are interested in learning about community, and shows up in people's social feeds when content from the community is shared.

That really is the primary value add that hosting your community on an existing social network brings. It makes it easier to attract and engage community members since they're already spending time there. But it comes at the cost of ownership of any member data that could help you improve your community experience and connect community engagement back to your business's systems of record. Growing a community on an owned platform is harder in the short run, but more sustainable in the long run. We'll talk more about selecting the right community platform in chapter 6.

Creating Intentional Barriers to Entry

It might seem counterintuitive, but making it a bit more difficult to join your community, or making it difficult to reach a certain status in your community, will tend to create a stronger sense of social identity and belonging for those members.

Effort justification is a concept in social psychology that stems from Leon Festinger's theory of cognitive dissonance.[2] It describes a person's tendency to attribute a higher value to an outcome that they had to work harder to achieve.

We see effort justification play out in a lot of social groups from military training, to pledging a sorority or fraternity, to converting to a religion, to trying out for a sports team. Groups that require a great investment of time, energy, or work in order to gain membership can become very strong social identities and highly committed communities.

Please don't start hazing your customers. But you can think about the requirements that someone needs to meet in order to join your community, or reach a status within your community.

To become an Airbnb "Super Host," there are a range of requirements that hosts must meet. They can't cancel bookings, they have to maintain a minimum rating, and they must reach a minimum number of bookings in order to qualify.

Yelp has a range of requirements as well around how many reviews a Yelp user must have in order to be invited into the Yelp Elite.

Our inclination is to make the process of joining our communities as easy as possible. But the easier it is to get into your community, the less value people may apply to membership.

Some communities take the simple step of adding an application to join the community. So you can't just sign up, you have to fill out a form and answer questions to essentially show that you are a good fit for the community. That simple process of having to apply can make people value membership more greatly, and feel confident that the group will be curated and safe since every member is vetted.

Other communities make their community open to anyone, but make it difficult to reach a specific status within the community. For example, anyone can join the CMX community, but you must apply and go through an interview to become a CMX Connect host and start hosting local events under the CMX brand.

The members of communities with higher requirements are very proud of their membership. When they meet another member, they feel an immediate connection to each other. It's because they all went through the same struggle to get there. They all had to earn it.

Designing a Compelling Onboarding Experience

Once you've recruited a member, you now get to onboard them.

Too many companies miss the opportunity to make their onboarding exceptional. They create a really bland welcome email for everyone who joins their community, that makes a bunch of asks of the person, and just hope that they'll become an engaged community member.

The first time someone joins your community is a critical opportunity for you to make a good first impression, have a successful first run through Social Identity Cycle, and make it more likely that the member will come back.

Our prehistoric brains are primed to make snap judgments about people and groups based on limited information. In the early days of humanity, being able to immediately determine if a person or group was trustworthy increased the likelihood that we would survive. We have the same brain today, and we make the same kinds of snap judgments that become very hard to change once someone has formed an opinion.

So you don't want to leave your first impression to chance. When designing an onboarding experience, I like to ask three questions:

1. What do you want them to know?
2. What do you want them to feel?
3. What do you want them to do?

For example, we personally welcome and tag every new member who joins the CMX Facebook Group and want them to ...

◆ *Know* our vision, values, and guidelines so that they get inspired about the larger reason we're all gathering, and understand a bit about the culture we're intentionally creating.
◆ *Feel* very welcome, like they just found a community that they know they can trust and that wants them to succeed. We want them to feel accepted, inspired, and energized.
◆ *(Do)* take the first step of introducing themselves and to start browsing the content in the community to get a good idea of what people talk about.

I'm confident that if they are the right fit for the community, and we can make them know, feel, and do those things, the odds of them becoming an engaged member of our community are very high.

Remember, when they first join, you don't want to make a big ask for them. It can be so small that it doesn't feel like much of an ask at all. And it should always be presented as something that will bring them value. When we ask new members to introduce themselves, we tell them that we'd love to learn more about what they're working on, and we ask them to share one challenge that they're working through currently so we can immediately start bringing them value. And we ask them to browse the content so they can start learning and getting a feel for the space.

Onboarding isn't just for new members! Every time a member levels up into a new group or identity, you have an opportunity to onboard them again. If someone reaches a Power User status like the Airbnb Super Host community, you can onboard them and think through what you want them to know, feel and do when they first get inducted.

Whenever a CMX community member gets approved as a CMX Connect Chapter Host, we onboard them into our host community, and provide them with lots of information, resources, and experiences to learn about the program and get them started on the right foot. They get access to our private channel just for hosts, we send them our playbook, and we give them a big shout-out in the community as a new host.

How to Move Members Up the Commitment Curve

Now that you've onboarded your new members, your next logical question is probably, "How do you get members to start participating and move farther up the commitment curve?" Good question! Thanks for asking.

My belief is that you generally can't *get* anyone to do anything that they aren't organically motivated to do. If they don't care about your community, or they don't get value from participating, you can't make them care.

But if they are motivated, there may be obstacles preventing them from moving up the curve. Maybe they feel ready to post in your Slack group, but they don't know what's considered acceptable yet. Or maybe they want to launch a local chapter, but they don't know what the time commitment would look like or how to go about getting set up as a leader, so they don't move up into the leadership level.

Take the time to talk to your members at each level of participation and learn more about their experience. Ask your passive members if they'd be interested in participating more actively, and why they haven't taken that leap yet. Ask your power members if they'd be interested in becoming a leader and why they haven't applied yet.

From those interviews, you'll start to identify the obstacles that you can help your members overcome with better education and communication. You can then build that education into your onboarding experience and your community resource documents.

You can also run campaigns with the specific intention of moving members into the next level of participation. My friend Suzi Nelson ran a highly successful campaign specifically focused on activating the lurkers in the community she managed for DigitalMarketer.com, called DM Engage. She called it the "Love Our Lurkers Week."[3] Every day for five days, she posted a new piece of content in the community focused on helping overcome obstacles that passive members have. The agenda looked like this:

- ◆ Day One: Posting Tips and Tricks
- ◆ Day Two: List of Legendary Posts
- ◆ Day Three: Meet Our Most Influential Members
- ◆ Day Four: Why Contribute to DM Engage
- ◆ Day Five: How Your Community Manager Can Help You

This campaign aimed to show passive members how to contribute in a quality way, what great contributions and members look like, the value they'd get by participating, and how they can find help if they need it.

The campaign was a wild success. Nelson was able to activate 44 percent of the lurkers in their community. Of the members who never participated in the community before, 11 percent made their first post, 17 percent made their first comment, and 16 percent initiated a reaction ("liked" a post).

You can take this same idea and apply it to any level of participation. If you want more members of the community to apply to be a local chapter leader, then you can run a campaign aimed at answering common questions about being a leader, spotlighting successful leaders, and communicating the value that leaders get out of their participation.

You never know who might be motivated to participate more in your community, and just needs a little push.

Toward the top of the commitment curve, a lot of companies will create an official program and a distinct identity just for their power users. For example, Airbnb created the Super Host program, Notion created the Notion Pros program, and eBay created the Power Sellers program.

By creating a unique identity for your power users, you give them a stronger sense of community, and you give members in the outer rings something to strive for (to become a member of the power user group).

You may not know what qualifies as a "power user" right away. Over time, as your program matures, the requirements will get more defined and you'll be able to better articulate it to your community.

Power User status creates a clear goal for members to strive for. Members of power user programs typically get access to a range of perks and benefits, like exclusive events, access to more features, swag, and a direct line of communication with the company. We'll talk much more about how to reward your members, and power users in the next Chapter.

Activating Successful Community Leaders

At the very top of the commitment curve of any great community, above even power user status, you're likely to find official leadership positions.

Taking on a leadership role is the ultimate form of contribution in a community. For someone to reach that level, they have to be so invested, so committed to the community, that they are willing to put in their time, energy, and resources to own some element of creating and facilitating the community experience.

One of the most common leadership programs is where companies empower members of the community to run a local chapter in their city, organizing events and experiences under the brand umbrella.

We've spoken about a few of these kinds of community programs already. Duolingo's 2600+ monthly language events are run by these kinds of local leaders. Google has over 1,000 Google Developer Groups around the world, Salesforce has hundreds of Trailblazer chapters, Rising Tide Society has over 400 chapters – all volunteer run and under the official stamp of the brand.

To ensure that your leaders can be successful, you want to provide them with as much guidance and support as possible. These programs always have some sort of playbook that guides leaders on what to do, what the expectations of the program are, and how to be successful.

You'll want to make your playbook as detailed as possible. I once reviewed the TEDx playbook that TED gives to its local organizers and it was well over 80 pages. TED events are highly produced and maintain a very high bar of quality, so they guide their organizers on everything from sponsorship policies, to speaker preparation, to stage design, and anything else they need to know to run a TEDx event.

They key to making these programs successful is to take away as much of the work and decision making as possible for your leaders.

Make it as easy as possible for them to host successful events, and to focus on the decisions that matter most for their local communities.

You'll also want to create a community space for your local organizers to connect and share tips with each other. Our CMX Connect hosts absolutely love to help us onboard new hosts, share lessons learned with each other, and constantly turn to each other for support. Your program will scale much more efficiently if leaders are able to support each other and exchange knowledge.

Where a lot of companies struggle to scale programs like this is when it comes to operations and data. If you have hundreds of local chapter leaders organizing their events on different tools, it becomes very difficult to ensure consistency across the program, and for you to access the data you need to understand who's RSVP'ing and attending your events. Ideally, you can host the entire program on, and have all of your local leaders using, one platform to centralize operations.

There are many other ways for community members to take on official leadership positions. Most large online communities empower loyal members to become official moderators, to help manage the community space. Again, this helps the community team scale their efforts in a way that would be impossible if they had to do it all themselves.

Moderator programs are also going to come with some sort of playbook and education. Make sure moderators have what they need to successfully manage the parts of the community they're responsible for, and teach them how to manage conflict, what to do when there's an issue they can't resolve, and how to take care of themselves so they don't burn out.

Most parts of your community that you want to keep hands on and personalized, but you can no longer handle yourself, can be handed off to community leaders. In the CMX community, we could no longer keep up with personally welcoming the hundreds of members who were joining every month. So we created an official "welcome committee" of community members who volunteer to welcome new members who are at the start of the commitment curve every week, and make sure each member gets a personal message.

Whenever you put someone in a leadership position for your community, you'll want to focus on quality over quantity. You don't necessarily want to make it very easy to become a leader. By having an application and interview process, or requiring some level of experience in the community, you can ensure that they're truly invested in the community. And in your application and interviews, you can validate that they're aligned with the values of your community. These leaders are going to be representing you and your brand, and they will be interacting directly with other community members, sometimes in difficult situations. If they're hosting local chapters, it will take a lot of hard work to get their community off the ground, and they'll need to have the right motivations and skills to get it done. Focus on quality over quantity when selecting leaders. It's much harder to ask someone to step down from their position than it is to vet them thoroughly in the first place.

Notes

1. D. R. Conner and R. W. Patterson, "Building Commitment to Organizational Change," *Training and Development Journal* 36, no. 4 (1982): 18–30.

2. Albert Pepitone and Leon Festinger, "A Theory of Cognitive Dissonance," *The American Journal of Psychology* 72, no. 1 (March 1959): 153, https://doi.org/10.2307/1420234.

3. Suzi Nelson, "How DigitalMarketer Activated 44% of Silent Community Members | Case Study," DigitalMarketer, March 18, 2020, https://www.digitalmarketer.com/blog/activate-community-members/.

Chapter 5

Validation, Rewards, and Incentives

We've now covered the first two stages of the Social Identity Cycle: *identification* and *participation*. The third stage, *validation,* is critical for closing the loop, reinforcing the social identity, and moving members up the commitment curve.

Validation is what tells our brains that an experience was positive and helps us form new habits of identifying with and participating in communities.

In this chapter, we're going to talk about all the different ways that you can reward your members and help them develop a healthy habit of coming back and participating for years to come.

Creating Habits with Rewards

It's absolutely critical that members feel validated and rewarded for their participation if we want them to come back and participate again.

When we experience a reward, it tells our brain that the experience was positive and that we should take that action again. In his book *The Power of Habit*, Charles Duhigg talks about the habit loop, which consists of three steps[1]:

1. Cue
2. Routine
3. Reward

97

Say you want to change your morning routine and replace the habit of snoozing with a habit of running. The alarm going off is your cue, hitting the snooze button is your routine, and the reward is more sleep. So your brain forms this automatic loop where you don't even think about it, you just hit snooze.

Habits are critical for building engaged communities as well, especially online communities. In Chapter 1, we talked about how community can help you own a topic in someone's mind. This occurs when your members have built a habit of coming back to your community any time they have a question related to the topic that your community is focused on.

For example, Sales Hacker wants to be the first place that members turn to when they have a question related to sales. If they have to find a new sales CRM software (the cue), they should immediately think, "I should ask the Sales Hacker community about this!" (the routine), and get feedback from other members (the reward).

These cues can be internal or external. In his book *Hooked*, Nir Eyal took the habit loop and applied it to social products on the internet to help us understand why people habitually use apps like Facebook and Instagram.[2] At first, Eyal explains, the cues will be external. Maybe you see a link to Instagram somewhere and you click it. Or maybe Instagram sends you a notification on your phone and that pulls in. These are external triggers because they're coming from outside your brain, and bringing you to take action (click the notification). Then you'll feel the reward (seeing an interesting picture of video), and maybe you make an "investment" like clicking the like button, commenting, or posting your own picture.

These external triggers keep people coming back to social platforms until they form an internal trigger. Internal triggers come from our own brain. They start happening when you've repeated the path enough times that your brain automatically goes through the routine in response to the cue.

For example, you think, "I'm bored," and before you know it, you've already whipped out your phone and you're scrolling through TikTok. Or you might think, "I wonder what's happening in the world," and without thinking, open up Twitter to start scrolling.

Community participation is driven by the same participation loop. A member will see an external trigger, like a notification or an email from you or your platform, and decide if they want to go to your forum, group, or event in order to get the promised value.

Over time, if they continue to show up in your community and feel rewarded every time, it will form a new path in their brain and they will start coming back organically, without you needing to prompt them. Your power users probably don't need to get many notifications, they've developed a habit of checking in on your community every day.

Now, we've seen social media addiction becoming a problem around the world. I certainly don't want to advocate for creating unhealthy habits that your members can't break. But individual communities, because they're so specific, are unlikely to become quite as addictive as the Instagrams and Facebooks of the world. Your members will come to your community to talk about something specific, to learn, and to grow together – not to just mindlessly scroll through selfies and dance videos. I believe if you've created a truly safe, authentic, and valuable space for people to gather, it's unlikely their habit of participation will be unhealthy.

But people won't come back to your community at all if they don't feel validated, and experience a reward, for showing up. People often leave this third stage to chance, and just hope that members will feel rewarded for their contributions. As we'll discuss in this chapter, there's a lot you can do as the community organizer to validate your members and make sure they're getting value.

Extrinsic vs. Intrinsic Motivations

Motivation comes in two forms: intrinsic and extrinsic.

Extrinsic motivations are things you do in order to earn a reward or avoid punishment, both things that are provided to us by external people or systems. Examples of extrinsic motivations for communities are things like point systems, badges, or getting a shout out from the community manager.

Intrinsic motivations are things you do because you genuinely enjoy and value doing them, regardless of the external rewards or punishments. Self-determination theory says that intrinsic motivation is driven by three things: competence, relatedness, and autonomy.[3] We can find all three in communities. People join communities to grow their skills and learn, to connect with other people, and are more likely to contribute when they feel a sense of ownership.

Of course, communities work best when members are primarily intrinsically motivated. It's a requirement for true, deep communities. You need members who are there not to receive external rewards, but because they genuinely care about the community and the other members.

But external rewards can be effective when used wisely. A very powerful form of extrinsic motivation in communities is social acceptance.

Imagine you move to a new city and your friend invites you to grab some drinks with a group of friends you haven't met before. After a couple hours, you decide that you really like these people. You hope they like you too. At the end of the night, you head home, and one of the friends texts you to tell you how awesome it was to meet you, that you fit right in, and they'd like to hang out again soon.

Best feeling ever? Might be!

It feels really good to be accepted into a new group that we care about! It's the same in your community. It can be highly impactful for a member who's relatively new to your community to get a note from you, or another member, letting them know that they're happy to have them in the community. That's the kind of validation that will make that person want to come back and keep participating.

You don't want to overdo it. Studies show that giving someone too much praise for taking a minimal action will actually reduce motivation. This is called the *overjustification effect*,[4] which explains that when an intrinsic motivation is replaced with an extrinsic motivation, it can actually reduce the intrinsic motivation that made the person take the action in the first place.

This is why you have to be careful with external rewards in communities. If your members are intrinsically motivated to help each other, and you start giving them points, money, or prizes for taking actions in the community, they may start focusing on the points instead of the good feelings they get from helping.

Ultimately rewards, whether intrinsic or extrinsic, are about how they make us feel about ourselves. Everything we as humans experience comes from within. The trigger may come from outside, but how we perceive it and respond to it will impact how we feel.

So when you give someone a reward, the question is:

- How does the reward make that person feel about themselves?
- Does it make them feel important because the reward was very personal and thoughtful?
- Does it make them feel bad about themselves because they had higher expectations?
- Does it make them feel accomplished because they had to do something specific to earn that reward?

Whenever you're using "external motivators" like gifts, money, points, badges, etc., think about how it will make that person feel. Think about the intrinsic motivations those rewards will drive.

Avoid Replacing Social Norms with Market Norms

The overjustification effect is especially prevalent in social contexts. That's because we look at all transactions in what behavioral economist Dan Ariely calls either "social norms" or "market norms."

When we do something to help a friend, or do something as a favor, we make the decision based on social norms. For example, if I ask a friend to help me move, they'll do it, for free, as a favor to me.

When we do something for money or some sort of prize, it shifts our brain into market norms. Now we consider how much time and effort it will take to offer the service, and determine if it's worth it for the reward. For example, if I pay movers to help me move, they're doing it for the money, not because they care about me.

When you bring market norms and extrinsic rewards into a situation that was driven by social norms, the market norm tends to replace the intrinsic motivation. For example, if I offered to pay my friends $100 to help me move, they will now ask themselves if that $100 is worth it for their time, thinking in market norms instead of social norms. In his book *Predictably Irrational*,[5] Ariely shares a fascinating example of this phenomenon:

> *A few years ago, for instance, the AARP asked some lawyers if they would offer less expensive services to needy retirees, at something like $30 an hour. The lawyers said no. Then the program manager from*

AARP had a brilliant idea: he asked the lawyers if they would offer free services to needy retirees. Overwhelmingly, the lawyers said yes. What was going on here? How could zero dollars be more attractive than $30? When money was mentioned, the lawyers used market norms and found the offer lacking, relative to their market salary. When no money was mentioned they used social norms and were willing to volunteer their time. Why didn't they just accept the $30, thinking of themselves as volunteers who received $30? Because once market norms enter our considerations, the social norms depart.

Now, extrinsic motivation isn't all bad and can be quite effective when used correctly. For example, research shows that when a prize is unexpected, like you surprising a member with a swag package in the mail, it does not have a negative effect on their intrinsic motivation. The reward feels like a genuine "thank you" when it's unexpected, and so the member will not start measuring their contributions based on how much swag they got.

You can also reward members by simply making sure they're aware of the positive impact their contributions have had on other members. They're intrinsically motivated to help other community members, but they may not always be aware of the impact they've had on the community.

For example, when working with Google on their G2G program, their goal was to motivate employees to teach classes for each other. Employees did this on a volunteer basis, because they genuinely cared about helping their fellow Googlers. But instructors wouldn't always get feedback from students on what they learned and how the class impacted them. So we made it a priority to make sure instructors would get an updates with feedback and kind messages from students who participated in their class. This extrinsic validation aligned with the intrinsic motivation of the instructors.

You want to avoid being overly transactional in the rewards you offer to volunteers. Reinforce the intrinsic motivations with praise, social validation, and other extrinsic rewards.

SNAP! A Framework for Effective Extrinsic Rewards

Holly Firestone, who ran the User Group Community at Atlassian and Trailblazer Community at Salesforce, came up with a nifty framework called "SNAP!" that I love to use for mapping out the different kinds of extrinsic incentives that can thoughtfully motivate your community members to contribute.

SNAP! stands for Status, Networking, Access, and Perks. You can use this framework to brainstorm new ways to reward the members of your community.

Status

Social status sits at the heart of community. We join communities where we see an opportunity to improve our status among a group that we care about. We tend to leave communities when there's no more status to gain or we've lost status and don't feel we can gain it back.

Every form of community has a status system either intentionally or unintentionally built in. Even groups or teams that intend to be totally flat will see leaders organically form and gain influence over the rest of the group. And just being a member of a community can signify someone's status to the rest of the world, like being a member of a professional association.

As a community builder, you can help shape and design that social status system. There are lots of different tools used in communities to communicate a member's status.

Badges are often used to show off a members' status, position, or accomplishments in a community.

Members might be able to accumulate points for taking actions within the community and get a higher score over time. Some communities will give members the power to award each other points for making a good contribution, like Reddit does with their "Karma" system.

Status can also be an official membership level that members can reach. like we often see in power user programs, like The Yelp Elite. You can create a more formal status structure that members aspire to be able to reach.

You can also help drive status for your community members outside of the community. For example if you're a professional community, inviting members to speak at your events, spotlighting their accomplishments, and helping them grow their personal brand will improve their status in their industry.

Networking

Of course, community is all about the people, and who members have the opportunity to interact with.

Your job when building community is to create experiences that help your members meet and interact with the right people who will be interesting and useful to them.

You may have a completely open community where everyone can meet everyone. But you can always reward members with more curated experiences. Perhaps you invite your most valuable members to a dinner, or facilitate a small group discussion for a select group of members.

From the moment someone joins your community, you have the opportunity to connect them with other members. Some communities will use a welcome committee, or a buddy system, to make sure that every new member is personally welcomed into the group.

Access

When your community members are users of your product, they'll be invested in how your product changes and evolves over time. They want to feel like they have influence over the direction of your business.

You can reward members by simply making them feel heard and inviting them to share their opinions and ideas with your team. You can take it a step further and host sessions with your executives or invite them to exclusive betas of your product.

Some communities will launch a mentor program, helping qualifying members get access to a mentor who has volunteered their time. Or perhaps you can bring in experts for private, invite-only sessions with small groups of your members as a reward for some sort of contribution.

Think about who your members would want to have access to, that they don't have access to today. It can be a truly powerful reward.

Perks

Perks can be things like free training, free tickets to events, free certifications, free professional development, discounts, and everyone's favorite branded reward: swag!

Great perks will not only elevate members' personal profiles, but they also encourage the behaviors you want to see more of in the community. If you provide training, those community members take what they learn and bring it back into the community by sharing insights, answering questions, increasing the value of their contributions.

Swag is obviously a popular reward. Giving your members a comfy T-shirt, a mug, a sticker for their laptop, or something else representing your community can be effective *if* that person genuinely cares about your brand.

I find that a lot of companies think about swag the wrong way. Too often, companies just slap their logo on a T-shirt and hope that their members will wear it around and spread awareness of the brand. In reality, you just gave them a really comfortable pajama shirt that will likely never leave their house.

Instead of thinking about swag as a billboard, focus on how the swag will make the member feel when they wear it or see it. It doesn't even have to have your logo, as long as they remember that it's a representation of your community, and a reminder of a positive experience. A beautifully designed piece of swag that people actually want can be more effective at reinforcing their sense of identity as a member, even if your logo doesn't show up anywhere.

The Thing about Gamification

When looking specifically at rewards that fall under "status," we're often talking about what's known as gamification.

Gamification is any system where points, badges, and other ranking systems are used to fuel engagement, or "gamify" participation.

The thing everyone gets wrong with gamification is that they think it can be used to spark engagement where there isn't already organic engagement. I've been asked on many occasions, "We aren't seeing much engagement in our forum. Do you think adding a gamification system would help?"

Bad news. If you're not seeing much engagement in your community now, adding points, badges, swag, levels, or perks won't be much help.

Why? Because gamification rewards like badges and points aren't status, *they're proof of status*.

Game design expert and cofounder of Game Thinking Academy Amy Jo Kim, PhD, sees this mistake made all the time. She explains that, "People who come from a marketing background look at games and see a set of extrinsic motivators and reward schedules that can be lifted out and plunked down elsewhere. That's understandable, because points, levels, status, and rewards are the atomic units of loyalty programs, a staple in the marketer's playbook."[6]

But that's not where the magic is, says Kim. "Trying to drive long-term engagement with extrinsic rewards is a fool's errand. If metrics and rewards are your main event, you've got a shallow and/or manipulative product that won't hold people's interest over time. Even worse, you might be dampening their creativity and enthusiasm without knowing it."

Remember, all rewards are all about how it makes us feel.

So those points I could get for posting in your community? Why should I care about them? I won't. Unless of course, I care how other people in the community perceive me, and the points serve as proof of my investment and status.

That T-shirt you made for me is really comfortable. I might wear it while I'm cleaning my house or chilling with ice cream in front of the TV. But for me to wear your logo outside in public, I have to identify as a proud member of your community, and be excited for others out in the world to see that I'm a member.

If you have engagement going in your community already, then gamification can truly accelerate things like throwing gasoline on an open flame. It can move people along the commitment curve faster. Creating a "power user" level shows new members what they can one day become if they contribute enough.

The key is to align the gamification system with the intrinsic motivations of your members.

"Well-crafted games are an artful blend of intrinsic pleasure and extrinsic scaffolding," says Kim. "They invite you to take a mini-break from daily life, and spend time (together) in an alternate, simplified reality. Pleasurable activities and the pursuit of mastery are the beating heart of this micro-world, and progress scaffolding (points, levels, badges, power-ups) serves to support and amplify these core activities."

One more word of caution...

Once you've created a measurement system for ranking the status of your members, they might do whatever they can to improve their status whether or not they're actually creating value for the community.

For example, if you reward members for posting in your community, a member might start posting a lot of quick, low-quality posts, just to get their numbers up. So you need to ensure that your gamification system is rewarding quality contributions.

One way to do that is with a peer-to-peer reward system where members choose when to give each other points. Reddit does this with its karma system. Incorporating human judgment into the system will help prevent the gaming of your gamification system.

What can be gamed will be gamed. So never consider your system locked in stone. Keep tinkering and evolving it to make sure it's working properly, and it's being used fairly.

Come for the Utility, Stay for the Unity

Often, people don't join communities for emotional connection to other people. They join communities to solve a practical problem or achieve a specific goal. It's only after they've been in the community for a while and got to know the other members that the emotional connection motivates them.

For example, you might join a basketball team because you want to get exercise and you enjoy the game. You won't care about the specific members of your team until you start playing with them and you get to know them.

Or you might work for a company because you want to get paid, learn new things, and grow in your career. You likely aren't going to join to make new friends. But once you get to know your colleagues and form friendships, you'll find it harder to leave the company, because you'll also be leaving your friends.

You might join a forum because you have specific questions that you want answered. You don't yet know the people in those communities, so you won't yet see the social value of the group until you're in there.

Of course, you might do some of those things in order to meet new people in general. But you won't feel invested in the specific people within the group until you get involved. It's only after you've participated in the community for some time that you start to feel connected to other members. That belonging will keep you around for a longer time, and may even become your primary motivator for participating in the community. You become invested in the success of other members. You feel a responsibility to the community. You feel like you belong.

This is especially true when building professional and customer-focused communities. Your members and potential members will likely have very specific challenges they're looking for help with. General "networking" value might be an influence on their joining your community but they're looking for solutions to their problems, first and foremost, not new friends.

There's all sorts of practical or nonemotional value that communities provide to people. We join communities to learn new skills, to get answers to questions, to grow our network, to be entertained, to get feedback and recommendations, to collaborate, to work with others to achieve a goal or fuel change, to have a space to vent, etc.

So if you're working to attract new members to your community, figure out the most important practical value that they'll get from the community, and focus on that more so than the emotional value. Tell them what problems you will solve for them. That's what will get them in the door.

Over time, once they start forming relationships and getting integrated into the social structure of the community, they'll feel more emotionally invested. That emotional connection will have a big influence on member and customer retention. It's much harder to leave a community, or switch a product, when your friends are all in that community or using that product. Your customers will be less likely to switch to a competitor if they feel like your community is *their* community.

Measuring Community Health and Engagement Using the Social Identity Cycle

Remember back in Chapter 1, we talked about the three levels of community strategy, and the metrics you can track to measure the business value of your community. We can now look at measurement on the second level of your strategy: The community level. (For a refresher on the Three Levels of Community Strategy, flip back to Chapter 1.)

On the community level, you measure the health and engagement of your community over time. You want to see if the Social Identity Cycle is working, if members are coming back, and if they're having a valuable, quality experience.

Going back to the solar system analogy, we can think of members like particles floating in outer space and their "sense of community" is like gravity, pulling them together to form planets, solar systems, and galaxies. Like particles in space, as they gather and form a more dense mass, the gravitational pull of that mass increases and attracts more particles.

That's why it's so important to not just focus on activity rates but also the quality and depth of interactions, or "network density". Analytics alone will only tell you so much. You need to complement that data with qualitative research using interviews and surveys. Ten super tightly packed particles will have a stronger gravitational pull than thousands of particles that are widely spaced and have less density. Getting 10 people together who form deep relationships will serve as a stronger foundation of community than getting 1,000 people together who will be loosely connected.

Analytics can also be misleading as someone might be participating consistently in your community, but not feel included or not be getting much value. Maybe your community is the best option they have, but it's not actually serving them in the best way possible.

You can measure community health and engagement by looking at each of the three stages of the Social Identity Cycle, answering the following three questions:

- *Identification:* Do members identify as a member of the community?
- *Participation:* Are members coming back and engaging consistently over time?
- *Validation:* Are members getting the value they expected from the community?

Identification

To measure *identification* use surveys and interviews liberally. You can ask members if they agree, on a scale of 1 (weakest) to 10 (strongest), with statements like:

I feel like this community was built for people like me.

I identify as a member of this community.

My values and beliefs align with the values and beliefs of the community.

Ask any questions that you feel will tell you if your members feel a strong sense of identity.

Anecdotally, look for evidence that members are adopting your community's expressions of identity. Are members putting your logo in their avatars or bios on other sites? Are they wearing your swag? Are they adopting the language of your community? Any tattoos out there?

These are all good signals that your members are identifying strongly with your community.

Participation

For stage two, you can measure participation rates using your community data and analytics. Common measures of online community activity are monthly active users (MAUs), which tracks how many people were active in your community in the past 30 days, or related metrics like weekly active users (WAUs). Sarah Hawk, the VP of Community at Discourse, recommends using what's known as "the stickiness ratio" to give you a good idea of how engaged your members are. To find your ratio, divide your Daily Active Users (DAU's) by Monthly Active Users (MAU's). So if you have 30 members take an action in your community today, and 100 took an action in the last 30 days, then your engagement rate, or stickiness, is 30%. If you see a 30% DAU/MAU rate, you're absolutely crushing it, says Hawk. "Our meta community is around 20% and it's highly engaged. I've run successful communities at around 8–10%."

These are similar metrics to what product and marketing teams use to communicate health and success. It's easy for folks to understand the health of community in these terms.

Those totals will give you an idea if more people are participating in your community, but it won't necessarily tell you if you're retaining your members. It could be a whole new batch of people participating every month. So look at repeat usage and track that over time. For example, you can track how many members have taken at least three actions in your community in the last 30 days. You can also break down metrics based on when members joined. For example, look at activity rates amongst members who signed up in the last 90 days and compare it to members who signed up in the last 30 days to get an idea of your dropoff rates.

For event-based community programs, look at repeat attendees as a measure of consistent participation.

While it's important to track the growth of your active members in the community, remember that your passive members matter, too, especially for communities focused on solving customer support and success problems. In her book *Working in Public,* Nadia Eghbal describes the four kinds of communities that exist based on her research into open source communities:[7]

1. *Federations:* larger groups where there are significant amount of contributors creating content
2. *Stadiums:* larger groups that are following and engaging around a single creator
3. *Clubs:* small groups where most or all of the members are contributing significantly
4. *Toys:* a simple idea for a new community or platform that's still very small and experimental

As you can see, each of these community types vary based on the size of the group, and how many members are actually contributing to creating content. For a club, you'd want to see high participation rates from all members. In a federation, it's a core group of contributors that you want to make sure are successful and happy. For stadiums, size does matter. If you want your most active creators to stick around, they need an audience to consume their content!

So while a lot of people will say that the total number of community members or attendees is a vanity metric, it's still a useful insight to bring into your measurement mix for a lot of communities. You should measure both: the number of core contributors who are most active in your community, and the growth of passive members.

This is why it's hard to come up with a one-size-fits-all standard for community health. Every community is different. There are way too many factors across communities to fairly compare them. Communities can be built on totally different platforms, for different member types, with different kinds of actions and interactions, and can all be starting from a different place in terms of the audience a company had before launching a community.

So don't concern yourself with comparing activity rates against other communities. Just start tracking your own engagement, and work to improve it month-to-month and year-to-year.

Validation

Finally, you have the third stage in the social identity cycle. There are lots of ways to measure how much value your members are getting out of your community.

The easiest way, much like identification, is to ask them! With surveys, you can ask members if they agree, on a scale of 1 (weakest) to 10 (strongest), with statements like:

- ◆ I feel welcome and included in this community.
- ◆ I've learned something new in this community.
- ◆ This community has helped me achieve my goals.

Whatever the value is that members expect from your community, ask them if they've been getting that value.

One more standardized way a lot of companies measure the value that members are getting from the community is with Net Promoter Score (NPS). This score is based on one question, "How likely are you to recommend this community to a friend or colleague?"

By collecting answers to that one question, and looking at the data altogether, a business can get a decent idea of how valuable their community is to members. They can also break down the responses into groups, so they could get an NPS score for each layer of social identity or activity. You might find that power users are getting a lot of value, but new members are not.

One thing to be mindful of in any community member surveying is selection bias. Selection bias just means that the people most receptive to taking the survey are the ones who will likely take it, meaning you won't have the most clear representative sample to apply to your entire population. You'll understand those who take the survey really well, but not really understand those who don't take it.

Caty Kobe, who was the global head of Scalable Customer Success at Square and is now an operations lead at Airbnb, has run a lot of surveys to better understand the health of her communities. She makes sure to counterbalance her surveys with non-survey methods to account for this selection bias. "For instance, when looking at whether or not a support community deflected cases we would also see if anyone who had posted had also created a case with our support team about the same topic within 72 hrs. Using their Single Sign On (SSO) ID as the connection between the two behaviors we were able to double check the survey responses of 'yes I found my answer' to how many cases were actually submitted to get a better understanding of our self-service rate."

You'll also want to control your data collection process to account for other factors that might influence the outcomes. "You can make sure you're not sending the survey during peak periods or low points of the year (that could skew some people from responding vs. others), making sure you're surveying folks from the same type of area / demographic, etc.," explains Kobe. For example, you might find that your community activity volume is trending low if you're looking at a week that tends to be seasonally low each year. Normalizing would remove that week and let you use the more consistent data to benchmark against.

Finally, it's important to tie your community engagement metrics back to the business outcomes you set out to achieve. This will ensure that you're not just building community for the sake of community.

To do this, go back to the commitment curve and find the actions that will drive the business objective you set for your program.

I call these *ROI actions*. An ROI action is any action that a member takes that you know is directly correlated to revenue or a key business objective.

We can use the SPACES framework in Table 5.1 and see what an ROI action might be that correlates to each part of the model.

TABLE 5.1   Valuable action in SPACES.

Business Objective	ROI Action Examples
Support	Answer a question for another customer.
Product	Share a piece of feedback or idea.
Acquisition	Refer a new customer or host an event that drives leads.
Contribution	Submit a piece of content.
Engagement	Renew a contract.
Success	Teach a class for other customers.

These are actions that will live somewhere on your commitment curve. By tracking the number of members who take that action over time, you can get a good signal of whether community engagement is driving business results.

Notes

1. Charles Duhigg, *The Power of Habit: Why We Do What We Do in Life and Business* (New York: Random House Trade Paperbacks, 2014).

2. Nir Eyal, *Hooked: How to Build Habit-Forming Products* (Norwick: Penguin Books, 2016).

3. Richard M. Ryan and Edward L. Deci, "Self-Determination Theory and the Facilitation of Intrinsic Motivation, Social Development, and Well-Being," *American Psychologist* 55 (1) (2000): 68–78, https://doi.org/10.1037/0003-066x.55.1.68.

4. Edward L. Deci, Richard Koestner, and Richard M. Ryan, "A Meta-Analytic Review of Experiments Examining the Effects of Extrinsic Rewards on Intrinsic Motivation," *Psychological Bulletin* 125 (6) (1999): 627–668, https://doi.org/10.1037/0033-2909.125.6.627.

5. Dan Ariely, *Predictably Irrational: The Hidden Forces That Shape Our Decisions* (New York: Harper Perennial, 2010).

6. Amy Jo Kim, Raph Koster, and Scott Kim, *Game Thinking: Innovate Smarter & Drive Deep Engagement with Design Techniques from Hit Games* (Burlingame, CA: Gamethinking.Io, 2018).

7. Nadia Eghbal, *Working in Public: The Making and Maintenance of Open Source Software* (San Francisco: Stripe Press).

Chapter 6

Designing Community Spaces and Experiences

Congrats, you've completed your Social Identity Cycle! You now know who your members are, how they will participate, and how to validate and reward them. And hopefully, you have some ideas of how you'll measure the health and engagement of your community. That gives you plenty to work with on the community level of your strategy. We're ready to move into the third and final level of your community strategy: the tactical level.

In this chapter we'll look at the spaces and experiences that you're creating for your community, and what you'll do day-to-day to make those spaces and experiences highly engaged. We'll talk about the different kinds of experience you can organize, go through the 7Ps of community experience design, and talk about the specific elements that can make your community experiences truly meaningful and memorable.

The Two Kinds of Community Experiences

Although there are a lot of actions a member can take along the commitment curve, the real community magic happens when they participate in a shared experience.

It's your job as a community builder to thoughtfully design spaces and experiences that draw your members in, make them feel at home, and serve as a proper environment for the kinds of interactions you want them to engage in.

115

All community experiences fall into two buckets: synchronous or asynchronous.

Synchronous experiences are where members are participating live, at the same time, usually in the form of an event or meeting. Think conferences, workshops, discussion circles, meetups, etc. These kinds of experiences can be virtual or in-person. They're great for helping members connect more intimately, have deeper conversations, and create serendipity.

Asynchronous experiences are where members interact without needing to be present in the space at the same time. Think forums, groups, messageboards, and chat groups. These kinds of experiences only happen online, and allow members to connect with the community 24/7. It's more accessible since people can connect from anywhere in the world at a time that is convenient for them. And it allows members to hold conversations with larger groups of people, collecting a wider variety of feedback and insights.

Most great communities I've seen have a combination of both. They offer asynchronous spaces for members to connect every day, get answers to questions, and engage in discussions. Then they'll complement those spaces with live events and gatherings where members get to interact in-person or virtually over video.

Asynchronous experiences provide breadth. Synchronous experiences provide depth.

Companies sometimes think of in-person or event-driven communities as hard to scale, but just look at the Duolingo example we spoke about earlier in the book. 2,600 events are being hosted per month around the world, by empowering members to self-organize. Virtual events like Google's DevFest gathered tens of thousands of developers around the world for over 200 simultaneously hosted events. Dreamforce, Salesforce's big conference, brought together over 70,000 attendees in San Francisco. Burning Man gathers close to 80,000 people in the desert, and has local "burns" being hosted all around the world year-round. Event-driven communities absolutely scale.

Bringing members together live enhances the asynchronous experience. Now when members interact on your forum, it won't just be an avatar but an actual person that they've met, talked to, and shared an experience with.

And online spaces will enhance your offline experiences by making sure members can stay connected, and continue to support each other in between live gatherings.

My recommendation, in most situations, is to do both.

Repetition, Repetition, Repetition

Music is the perfect metaphor for facilitating community engagement. A great song will have a steady beat with different lyrics, a chorus where everyone knows the words to sing along, and a crescendo where the energy peaks and the crowd goes wild.

A great community is the same. It will have a steady cadence of different content and experiences for people to engage with (the beat), regular rituals where everyone knows how to participate (the chorus), and then one or two big energizing experiences every year where the whole community comes together (the crescendo).

The key is repetition and consistency. When your members can experience your community in a consistent, repetitive way, it will make it easier for them to develop a habit of coming back and they'll know exactly what to expect and how to participate.

A simple way to do this is to create standard, recurring experiences. Keep the overall format of the experience the same, and host it at the same time every day, week, month, quarter, or year.

A brainstorming exercise I often take companies through will help you come up with ideas for recurring experiences you can host for your community, based on different time frames. You can do it yourself or with your team by writing out across the top of a piece of paper the following time intervals, as shown in Figure 6.1.

DAILY   WEEKLY   MONTHLY   QUARTERLY   ANNUALLY

FIGURE 6.1

Under each interval, write down at least three ideas for what you can do to engage your community with a recurring experience daily, weekly, monthly, quarterly, and annually.

If you look at any great community, there's a good chance they have experiences hosted at all, or almost all, of these frequencies.

A general rule is that the less frequent the experience is hosted, the bigger the production it will be.

Consider most religions for example:

- ◆ *Daily:* Members pray at home.
- ◆ *Weekly:* They go to their place of worship to gather and pray together.
- ◆ *Monthly:* There's an event, a fundraiser, or some other sort of gathering.
- ◆ *Quarterly:* There's usually a holiday every three months or so.
- ◆ *Annually:* There's a big holiday that brings everyone together.

These rituals are consistent year to year. Everyone knows when they are and they already plan on participating. The format is the same each time, but still leaves room for creativity and exploration within the format the makes it more exciting for members.

Figure 6.2 shows some of the ways this cadence shows up in the CMX community:

- ◆ *Daily:* We start and facilitate discussions in our online community.
- ◆ *Weekly:* We have recurring threads like our New Member Welcome on Mondays, Promoday on Wednesdays, and Friday Fundays.
- ◆ *Monthly:* We host a local event on the first Tuesday of every month, and have dozens of chapters around the world who do the same.

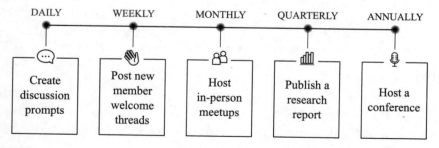

DAILY	WEEKLY	MONTHLY	QUARTERLY	ANNUALLY
Create discussion prompts	Post new member welcome threads	Host in-person meetups	Publish a research report	Host a conference

FIGURE 6.2

- ◆ *Quarterly:* We do a big study with the community and publish a new research report.
- ◆ *Annually:* We host CMX Summit and CMX Global, our two large conferences.

So you can see, on a daily level, the experiences are more minimal (prayers, discussions) and as the timeframe gets larger, the experiences are bigger and more produced (events, holidays, conferences).

Now not all communities need to focus on all of these time frames. Burning Man, for example, hosts one epic event per year and that's pretty much it! It's such a powerful experience, though, that people spend all year preparing for it, creating artwork, fundraising, and gathering with their friends and camps. So even though the organizing body of Burning Man only does the one event, the community has created its own recurring experiences throughout the year to keep getting together. And of course, the community also started organizing their own local "Burns" around the world.

So don't worry if your community doesn't have content and experiences for all of these time frames. Just use this template as a way to brainstorm ideas for how you can create more consistent recurring experiences for them to engage with.

Consistency is incredibly important in communities. It's much easier for members to engage when they know that we welcome new members every Monday, that a meetup is going to happen on the first Tuesday of every month, and that our conference happens around the same time every year. It helps them build a habit of coming back consistently. It's already on their calendar. They have to do less guessing about what's going to happen when.

These kinds of recurring experiences aren't only valuable for helping members form habits, they deepen their connection to the shared identity over time. When they show up to an event and they know what the format, flow, and rituals will be, they feel like they're "in the know." When I show up to temple for Yom Kippur, I know the order of operations as I walked in the door, put on my tallis, and went through the prayers in the same order that they do every year. I know I'm going to fast for 24 hours, and that I'm going to absolutely demolish some bagels when the sun goes down. These are our rituals.

When someone comes to CMX Summit who's been there for 10 conferences in a row they feel a sense of pride and familiarity. They feel like an established member of the community. They know the rituals and regular experiences that show up at every event. They know we always have "birds of feather" discussions, where we set up lots of round tables, each one with a different topic, and attendees can just sit down and start discussing that topic. They know we'll have an "introvert zone," a talk-free space our former CMX Summit lead Evan Hamilton created to provide attendees an opportunity to quietly hang and get some alone time. They know that every speaker will get a massive heartfelt standing ovation when they get on and off the stage because we do it every year.

Of course, not everything in a community will be recurring and repetitive. Having variable content and experiences is important, too. It keeps your members on their toes and makes them want to come back to see what they might have missed. While CMX Summit happens around the same time every year, we don't want the experience to be exactly the same. Members won't feel as compelled to come back if it were the same content, the same exact experiences, the same people, etc. So every year, we come up with new creative experiences and content to mix things up and surprise and delight our members. If a new experience works well, it might just become another staple in the CMX community.

The 7Ps of Community Experience Design

Once you have a good idea of the types of experiences you want to create for your community, whether they're synchronous or asynchronous, and recurring or one-offs, the next step is to design the experience itself.

When designing any shared experience, there's a standard set of pillars we use called The 7Ps:

- ◆ *People*. Who are we gathering?
- ◆ *Purpose*. Why are we gathering?
- ◆ *Place*. Where are we gathering?
- ◆ *Participation*. What will participants do?

- ◆ *Policy*. What are the rules and guidelines?
- ◆ *Promotion*. How will you invite members?
- ◆ *Performance*. What will success look and feel like?

If you're launching a new forum, use the 7Ps to design your experience first. When you want to host a new kind of event for your community, you can design it with The 7Ps. Any experience you create for your community, The 7P's will be your guide.

Example of The 7Ps: Tuesdays Together

Earlier in the book, I referenced Honeybook's amazing community, Rising Tide Society. One of the pillars of their community is an format called Tuesdays Together, a meetup on the second Tuesday of every month where creatives and entrepreneurs gather together for coffee and conversation. Here's a brief overview of how Natalie Franke, the founder of Rising Ride, mapped out the 7Ps for these incredible community events!

People Tuesdays Together meetups are gatherings for small business owners who have a desire to share their knowledge, learn from their peers, and grow together. The events are organized by local industry leaders in the community, and are focused on gathering creatives and entrepreneurs, including: Artists, Bloggers, Boutique Owners, Calligraphers, Designers, Event Planners, Florists, Makeup Artists, Photographers, Stylists, Wedding Pros, Writers, and more!

Purpose We believe that getting out from behind your computer and building true relationships with other creative entrepreneurs is an incredible tool for success. By joining a Tuesdays Together meetup, community members can expect to learn new business tips directly from their colleagues, grow in confidence, and find a network of compassionate professionals in their local area.

Place Meetups occur on the second Tuesday of the month at local coffee shops.

Participation Meetups will vary from city to city and each leader has the freedom to cultivate gatherings that best fit their local area. However, most gatherings include a discussion on the topic of the month followed by an open question and answer segment. We encourage all attendees to not just attend and listen but to actively participate in the discussion.

Policy Every meetup is designed to be approachable, authentic, and uplifting, and embody the five Rising Tide values:

1. People come first.
2. We go the extra mile.
3. We love what we do.
4. We are fearless.
5. We are family.

Leaders also agree to the Rising Tide community code of conduct, are expected to uphold the values, and act in accordance with the Rising Tide mission in-person and online.

Promotion Local leaders promote their events and grow their local communities over time by inviting members to their local Facebook Group.

Performance A successful Tuesdays Together meetup will receive positive reviews from attendees in a post event survey.

The 7Ps Keep Communities Engaged

This is a brief example of a 7P design, and a full 7P plan can go into much more depth. But even briefly, you can see how designing for each of these elements can give you a more clear idea of what a space or experience will look and feel like, and help you get clarity on the focus, intention, and expected outcomes of the space or experience.

Each Rising Tide Leader could use the 7Ps to get more specific in designing local events and experiences. They could use it for defining the key elements of local Facebook Groups that the leaders use to keep their communities engaged in between events.

Wherever and however you're bringing your community together, the 7Ps can help you get the experience just right. Now let's dive into the pillars of the 7Ps in more depth and explore other keys to creating highly engaging spaces and experiences.

Curating the Right People for the Right Purpose

It always starts with people. When designing any community experience, the first thing you should think about is who you're going to be bringing together and why.

Our temptation is often to make events and spaces open to anyone, or at least everyone in our community. But like we discussed in Chapter 3, there are a lot of different identities in your community. Each of those identities may have unique needs, goals, and reasons for gathering.

So who are you going to invite into this space or experience, and why?

One way to get more specific about who you're inviting to participate in an experience is to start with your business goal in mind:

- ◆ If your goal is to improve customer retention and success, then perhaps you'll want to create an online group just for your customers to support each other.
- ◆ If your goal is to drive word of mouth and referrals, then you can organize a dinner and invite both your most loyal customers and your biggest target prospects so that they can sit and talk to each other.
- ◆ If your goal is to get more insight for your product, you might want to invite members who have experience using your product to share their experience and tips with each other.

Your purpose can also be tied to the kind of interaction and relationships you hope to be able to facilitate:

- ◆ If your hope is to facilitate a very practical conversation, then think about who can you invite to the space who has deep experience with the topic you'll be discussing.
- ◆ If you want to make people feel like they're a part of something really big and exciting, then it may make sense to bring *everyone* together for a large event. Customers, prospects, audience members, employees, partners ... everyone.
- ◆ If you'd like to host a deep, vulnerable conversation, then you might want to only send private invitations, and choose people that you know will be respectful and personally invested in the topic.

Large events and online spaces are still going to be made up of many smaller spaces and experience. So you can still break it down into more specific spaces with an intentional purpose and group of people. Perhaps you host a VIP dinner for your customers at your conference. Or you create an "anonymous questions" section in your forum. Any identity that exists in your community is an opportunity to create an intentional, dedicated space.

We have a whole range of spaces and experiences where our community gathers at CMX and Bevy. We have spaces just for Bevy customers. We have spaces just for our CMX Connect chapter leaders to interact and support each other. We have free communities open to the entire industry, and premium spaces for paying members focused on enterprise communities. We have big global conferences, medium-sized local meetups, and small curated discussion groups. Every space has a unique purpose, focused on serving a specific group of people.

Whatever you organize, always start with people and purpose.

Aligning Size with Purpose

While it's common to want to grow your community, adding more people to a community space or experience isn't always a good thing.

A person will be much more willing to be vulnerable in small groups where they know and can see everyone who's listening and there's an expectation of confidentiality. If they were sitting on a stage in front of 1,000 people, they aren't going to be as open and vulnerable.

The smaller the group, the more safe the members will feel. So if you want to create a community experience where people can be vulnerable, share emotions or secrets, and be really open, you'll want to keep your group small. Smaller groups also mean that there's more visibility into who's in the group and how much they're contributing. Going back to Nadia Eghbal's classification of communities, "clubs" or small groups will have higher participation rates.

For other communities, bigger can be better. More members means more access to knowledge. It (usually) means a more diverse group of people to share insights. More opportunities for collaboration. If your goal is to help members get answers to questions quickly and efficiently, you're going to want a lot of experts in the community who can help them out.

Bigger can also make members feel like they're a part of something really exciting and important. The Women's March was one of the largest protests in the history of the United States. It's sheer size made them feel like they were a part of a meaningful and impactful community.

You can offer a diversity of experiences for your members, big and small. Don't take on organizing too many experiences at once, but consider that you might have many different kinds of people in your community who prefer different kinds of participation. Some members might like participating in a big forum, and some will prefer smaller online mastermind groups. Some will like attending big conferences and others will prefer getting together for a dinner. Online or offline, big or small, passive or active, you can offer a range of different experiences for your members to get involved in the way they need at that time.

I've found that people generally crave the size of community that they don't have. When our network spreads too thin, we crave intimacy. But intimate groups lack diversity and are slow to change, so we start to feel isolated and seek more options. It ebbs and flows.

Small groups → big groups → small groups.

Move from suburban → urban → suburban.

Focus on family → friends → network → friends → family.

Gather in small meetups → big conference → small meetups.

Small cults → big religion → small cults.

Inner circle → outer circle → inner circle.

If there are only small events focused on a topic, you probably have an opportunity to build a large gathering.

If there's only large gatherings, try building a smaller, more intimate group.

Today social media feels too broad and unsafe, so people are seeking more focused, independent communities. One day we'll feel siloed again and want to connect with larger networks.

Smaller groups provide the opportunity for more intimacy, but less diversity. Larger groups provide the opportunity for more diversity, but less intimacy. We tend to need both diversity and intimacy throughout our lives.

One last note on choosing the right size for your community: Whatever size group you choose to bring together for an experience, make sure you choose a space that's the right size for that group.

Online, a forum with 10 people in it will feel empty, and a chat group with 1,000 in it will feel extremely overwhelming. Don't launch a forum for 10 people. And don't squeeze 1,000 into a single chat feed.

Offline, putting 400 people in a space designed for 1,000 will make your event feel empty, and poorly attended. Put that same group of 400 people in a space designed for 350, and it will feel sold out and in-demand.

The size of your space is *really* important.

If I find a space is too big for my in-person event, I'll figure out ways to shrink the space. Put up partitioned walls or pipe-and-drape to make the space smaller. Move all the furniture so that it's bunched up in a tighter space rather than spread out around the room.

Online, there's not much you can do to hack a space when the numbers aren't right. Just make sure not to overwhelm a tool built for small groups with large numbers, and make sure you have enough people in your forum or group to make it feel full and active. 150 members is a good start for a lot of forums and Facebook Groups. Don't start off with too many subgroups and sections. Get critical mass in a few first, then add more spaces over time.

Choosing Community Software Platforms

One of the most common questions companies have is, "What platform should we host our community on?"

In fact, this is often the first question companies ask. They go straight to looking at community software platforms before really understanding their overall community strategy, and their goals for the specific space or experience they're organizing.

Your software platform isn't your community. Your software platform, like a physical venue, is just a place where your community gathers. Your people and the relationships among them are the community. And your goal will be to design spaces that are exciting, functional, and accessible for your members.

You'll find three levels of community software platforms:

Level 1: Free tools on existing social platforms (Facebook, LinkedIn, Slack). They cannot be customized, and there is limited or no access to member data. The big benefit is that since members are already there, it's easier to keep them engaged and bring them back into your community (Cost: Free).

Level 2: Low-cost tools that you can host on a subdomain and own the data. There are limited customizability and integrations. They offer a middle ground of customization and data ownership, without costing an arm and a leg (Cost: $1k–$10k/year).

Level 3: Enterprise-grade tools that are expensive, but fully customizable and have lots of integrations. You'll generally need developers and designers to help you build these spaces out, or that will be built into the cost of the software (Cost: $10k–$100k/year).

Some companies choose to build instead of buy. Usually, these are companies where the product *is* the community, like IndieHackers, the Ministry of Testing, and Product Hunt. It's really important for these kinds of indie communities to make their experience feel really unique and to have full control of the experience. For companies that have a product that isn't a community, it's generally recommended to buy instead of build, as developing and maintaining a community platform is usually very expensive and time consuming.

There's a whole range of criteria you can use to make a decision on community software. Here are a few I recommend getting clarity on before choosing your platform:

User Experience:

Does the platform feel intuitive and easy to use?

Is the design customizable, and can you make your community space feel like a unique home for your members?

Does it service the business purpose of the community, helping members take the "ROI action" that will drive results (e.g., if your community objective is "Support," will the platform make it easy for members to answer questions for each other and efficiently find the right answers to their technical questions?)

Data and Integrations:

Will you be able to tie community data to customer data?

Will you be able to integrate the platform with other tools you're using, and set up single sign-on (SSO)?

How does the platform protect user data and have they gotten an external audit of their security practices?

User Habits and Engagement

Are members already engaged on the platform (Facebook, Slack, email) or will they have to start using a new tool?

How are members notified of activity and brought back into the community?

Where will the community live? (e.g., onsite, mobile app, subdomain)

Information Architecture

How important is it for your members to find existing questions and answers?

Do you need to convert conversations into knowledge-base articles?

Do you want to optimize for conversational format or a structured Q&A format?

Budget

How much are you willing to spend on the software?

How much will it cost to build or customize the community?

How does the platform determine pricing and how much do you expect the cost to grow over time?

Those are just some of the questions you can ask as you do a full vendor review of community software platforms. I've seen much longer lists of questions. Just make sure you're asking the right questions that will help you feel confident that your platform will serve both your members' and your business's needs.

For a full review of the community platforms out there, take a look at the CMX Guide to Community Platforms, which is available for free online (https://cmxhub.com/cmx-guide-to-community-platforms/).[1]

Should You Host Your Community on a Free Social Network?

There's a common debate on whether companies should build community using tools and spaces that they control, where they can optimize the experience and own the data, or build the community on an existing platform (like Facebook, Reddit, Slack, or LinkedIn) where people are already engaged, but they don't have control of the experience or access to member data.

For a brand new community, it's wise to tap into the existing networks. Go to where your customers are spending time. Make it easy for them to connect, to get support, and participate in the community.

You can host spaces on both social platforms and on your own, owned platform. Some companies use social platforms to host their "interest-based" communities, and host their customer-support communities on their own site. Then when someone asks a more technical question in the social platform, they can direct them to their forums.

Yes, you won't have the data if you host your community on Facebook. You can't measure everything. That doesn't mean it's not valuable. CMX has more than 10,000 people interacting in its Facebook Group. We don't know exactly who's in there, but it's such an engaged space that whenever we announce a new product, or want to drive people to an event, we know we can reach a lot of members in that space.

We can also track how traffic from the Facebook Group leads members to sign up for products and spaces where we do own the data. So the group serves as a good "top-of-the-funnel" space that engages members until they're ready to make a bigger commitment.

There's a good chance, if you have a popular brand, that you won't have a choice. Your community members will self-organize their own communities on existing social platforms. The kneejerk reaction a lot of companies have to this is to freak out and send a legal-sounding email to the organizers that they have to shut the group down. I highly recommend not taking that approach. It's a *really good* thing that your members want to organize around your brand. Embrace it. Empower those leaders. Support them. Show up in a positive, friendly light in those spaces.

Your community is not your software platform. Your community is your people. You can explore lots of different ways to bring together the people in your community. Some will want to participate in your owned forum. Others will prefer to join a subreddit or a Facebook group started by another customer. You can't control where your people gather. You can suggest, and nudge them, but they're going to go where they're going to go.

Having access to community data and being able to connect it back to your CRM is *very* important, especially for businesses who are working to connect community activity back to revenue data. But don't overrotate on controlling everything. The most important thing is that you're creating relationships, connections, and engagement amongst your community.

Connect your customers wherever they want to connect.

Designing Spaces That Make People Feel Seen

Getting specific about who you're gathering and why you're gathering them will help educate the many small decisions you make when you design your community spaces and platforms. With intention, you can create a space that makes your members feel like this was a place made just for them.

In a physical space, there are a great deal of opportunities to communicate who your community is for. At Ethel's Club, Naj Austin brought a ton of intention when she designed the coworking space. "People of color aren't used to seeing themselves in corporate settings and coworking spaces. So we wanted to design everything in the space to make our members feel like it was created just for them," says Austin.

She wanted Ethel's Club to be a place where members felt seen for who they are. Every book on the bookshelf was written by a person of color. All the art was created by artists from underrepresented groups. And my favorite part: the mirrors. She intentionally put mirrors all around the space, explaining, "I wanted them to literally see themselves in a space that was specifically designed for them."

That attention to detail translated into their website and online community as well. Everything you see on the Ethel's Club website communicates who the community is for and the culture you can expect when you join. All the pictures are of people of color in the creative industry. And when you scroll to the bottom of the website, you'll find a spinning record and a link to Ethel Club's Virtual Vibes, a Spotify playlist of tunes curated for the community. Everything is designed to make members feel seen.

What do you want your community space to feel like?

◆ Do you want a space that feels modern and innovative because that's the identity of your community members?
◆ Or do you want it to be cozy and safe, so you can host more intimate discussions?
◆ Do you want people to feel relaxed in your space or energized?
◆ Do you want them to be productive or do you want them to just chill?

Take the time to really think about who you're gathering and why you're gathering them. Let that inspire how you want your space to feel.

Starting with a BANG!

There are two ways that communities generally get started.

Some start with a small group, and then grow gradually, organically from there. Others kick off with a bang, with a large event that gives the community a big initial burst of energy, like a jolt to get the engine going.

I spent years working on community teams, writing about my learnings, and developing a network of community professionals before starting CMX. And I cofounded TheCommunityManager.com where we built a strong reputation and audience. So in some ways, I was already building the CMX community long before we ever hosted our first event. But when we did start CMX, we kicked it off with CMX Summit, a big premium conference with speakers, sponsors, catering, networking events … the works.

I can't claim to have known what I was doing at the time, but the effect that this had is clear looking back. By bringing together 250+ community professionals for a big, first-of-its-kind event that people loved, it lit a fire that has been burning ever since.

Attendees felt energized by the experience, motivated to work in the field and to continue to connect and learn. The first CMX digital community was the Facebook Group that we created for attendees to talk to each other. It had so much energy and engagement in the weeks leading up to the event and at the event because of the build-up that big events create. After the event, we decided to keep the group going, and open it up to other community professionals who weren't at the event. This became CMX Hub, the digital home for our community to connect, growing to thousands of members over the next six years.

If we started CMX with another small online group, or a smaller meetup, I don't think it would have worked. It's not what the people in the industry needed at the time. There were some great events out there, but none in the United States that went as high production with speakers and content as we did. The industry needed a big boost of energy, and the conference did that.

Companies use this technique when launching or increasing engagement in online communities as well. The asynchronous nature of forums makes it hard to feel like there's a lot of energy pulsing through the space in the early days. So they host big events on the forum to get everyone to sign on at the same time and participate in a big shared experience. It could be as simple as a series of Ask Me Anythings (AMAs) where you invite experts to show up in the community and answer questions for an hour. Or it can be a week-long content series like the "Love Our Lurkers Week" that Suzi Nelson organized for the Digital Marketer community.

These kinds of bigger swings can kick off a new community with a bang, or amp up the engagement and energy in an existing community.

Creating Peak Moments

It turns out that you only need one really impactful moment for a member to look back fondly at their community experience.

Think back to the last big, exciting experience you had. It could be a music festival you attended, a wedding, a vacation you took. What do you remember?

Chances are, you don't remember every little detail of the experience; you only retained the most exciting, most scary, most energized, or most surprising moments. You only remember the "peak" moments.

In their book *The Power of Moments,*[2] Dan and Chip Heath teaches us that when people think back to experiences they have, it's only these peak moments that they retain.

If you go to Disney World, they explained, the memories of waiting in long lines and spending a lot of money on food isn't what pops into your head months and years later. The moments you remember are the high points, watching the fireworks, flying through Space Mountain, meeting Mickey Mouse, seeing the parade go by.

This is a critical lesson for community builders. When you're creating your online community experience or hosting a big event, 99 percent of the details that you're sweating over will not be what people will remember. They'll only remember the absolute best and absolute worst experiences they have.

How can you build positive peak moments into your community?

A lot of communities stay relatively consistent in their experience. Online, there are questions and answers, discussions, and knowledge sharing. When members think about their experience in a forum, it's mostly unremarkable.

Sometimes it's out of your control. Serendipity has a way of pulling peak experiences out of thin air: a spontaneous run-in with someone that ends up becoming a close friend; the right conversation that leads to a new job.

I remember at the South by Southwest (SXSW) festival one year, I was walking by myself to a networking event when I passed by a bar that had a blackboard sign that said "Local Natives Live @ 7:30!" Local Natives was one of my favorite bands but still relatively unknown at the time (+1 hipster point for me). I looked at my watch and it was 7:00 p.m. The bar was still empty. I walked in and asked the bartender, "Are the Local Natives actually playing here in 30 minutes?" and she said "yes!" I ordered a beer and posted up next to the stage as the place filled up behind me over 30 minutes until the band came out and I was treated to one of the best shows I've ever seen live in my life. Completely spontaneous! I can't tell you which speakers I saw that year, who I met, or really much of anything else I did at SXSW that year. But I'll never forget that serendipitous peak moment, and it's given SXSW a special place in my heart forever.

SXSW is famous for that kind of serendipity that happens when you put thousands of musicians, technologists, and leaders in a small city filled with great bars and music venues. I've been to the festival several times now, and every time, there was a random peak moment that kept me coming back next year.

Peak moments can take many different forms. They fall into a few different categories, laid out by the Heath brothers:

- *Elevation:* that top of the roller coaster, standing ovation, high-energy moment.
- *Pride:* the feeling of accomplishment, getting the spotlight, accomplishing a big goal.
- *Insight:* learning something new, getting that *ah-ha!* moment.
- *Connection:* meeting someone new or forming a deeper relationship with someone.

At CMX Summit, we try to create opportunities for all four:

- *Elevation.* Every speaker at CMX Summit gets a standing ovation when they get on the stage. We make the audience practice at the start of the day. These high energy moments make the event the speakers never forget and puts the audience in a great mood.

◆ *Pride*. We aim to use the CMX Summit stage to give a platform to underrepresented voices and up-and-coming professionals in the industry. For some, it's their first time publicly speaking and a huge moment of pride. We also spotlight our community leaders throughout the event.

◆ *Insight*. With all the amazing content at our event, it's rare that someone will leave without at least one really big *ah-ha!* moment for something they can apply to their own community.

◆ *Connection*. We create a range of different networking opportunities from speed networking to discussion groups to parties to increase the odds of new relationships forming. But let's face it, most relationships form at the bars and restaurants after the conference finishes.

Think about how you can design your community experiences to increase the odds that someone will have one of these peak moments. They'll never forget it.

Facilitating Small-Group Discussions

Small-group discussions are one of my favorite kinds community experiences to organize. They give you an opportunity to connect with people at a depth you just can't reach in larger or more public spaces.

One of the best community experiences I've ever had was a weekly lunch hosted at a small indie coworking space called Fabric, where I was a member.

Every Wednesday, we'd sit down for lunch and have a 90-minute discussion facilitated by the founders Chad Hamre and Brendan Baker. The format was simple: we'd go around and each share a high and low from our week for the first 45 minutes, then switch to a shared discussion on a single topic. It was a highlight of my week. It was a space I came to rely on, to reflect on my week, and it made me feel much more connected with my fellow coworkers. I've worked in many different coworking spaces in my career, and most of them just hope that members will get to know each other by being in the same building. Fabric made sure of it.

One week I invited my friend Ivan Cash, an artist, to participate in a Fabric lunch. He loved the format so much, he decided that he needed to start a discussion group for his network of creative founders. Since everyone lived in different cities, he decided to host virtual discussion groups. They decided on a monthly format and to focus on sharing highs and lows, giving each member a chance to ask for feedback on a challenge. The group has now been running for over a year and became another staple in my life.

That's why small discussion groups have become one of my favorite formats for building community. Hosted regularly, they become a deep and meaningful part of people's lives. They're genuine, and intimate. Something about having a small group of people listening makes people feel like they can be more open and vulnerable. Small groups allow for "real" conversations to happen, and ensures that everyone has a chance to have their voice heard. And the networking value is huge. I've met so many high-quality humans, and formed lasting relationships, through discussion groups.

These are things you just don't get in a big conference or webinar, or in an online group or forum. People are more reserved in those settings. They never know who's in the audience listening. In a small group, you know exactly who's there.

Now, small-group discussions have been happening in-person since the first time humans gathered around a fire. But now we have virtual discussion groups. They're IN the computer. No matter how much you optimize the experience, a virtual discussion group won't be the same as an in-person group. But, BUT!, you'll find that when done correctly, they're not all that different either and can have some unique advantages.

Whether you're gathering online or in-person, there are a number of formats you can use to make your discussion group really engaging and impactful.

First, for any event I host (big or small), I like to have everyone "arrive" in the space. Everyone's coming from another meeting, another task, a day of work, a different place, and then suddenly they're all in one room with a new group of people. By having everyone "arrive," they can feel present in the new space together, and leave the rest of their day behind them. You'll have more present, more focused attendees as a result.

There are lots of ways to have people arrive in your space. Scott Shigeoka, EIR at GoDaddy, likes to use breathing and mindfulness exercises. "Noticing your breath or another mindfulness exercise like imagining the little details in your day from the moment you woke up to getting to the meeting helps people feel more present." You can start by simply asking everyone to take three deep breaths together, and counting them out. "If you present it well, it doesn't have to feel *woo woo*," says Shigeoka. "I've done this even in more conservative spaces. It helps people feel more present and mindful, which is helpful for anyone in any moment of gathering."

For virtual events I like to kick off with a "ceremonial closing of tabs." I hit a singing bowl a few times while asking everyone to close their email, close out of their tabs, and remove any distractions.

You can also have people arrive in the space by asking members to say hello to a neighbor, all making a sound together, or anything else that makes everyone feel aware of their current environment and takes their mind away from whatever they were doing before.

Once everyone is engaged, there are a lot of different formats for kicking off and facilitating small-group discussions. Here are a few ideas I've used with success:

Round of intros: Kick off with a round of intros. Spice it up with a "fun" question like, "What cartoon character do you most identify with?"

Whip-around: An initial question that everyone answers to get everyone involved in the conversation early. A lot of these formats can be considered *whip-arounds*. They're usually quick answers to a question like, "What is your goal for this discussion?" or, "What is one thing you're grateful for?"

Traffic light: Ask everyone to share how they're feeling at that moment, "red, yellow, green."

High-and-low: Have each person share a high and a low from their life/work. This is also called "a rose and a thorn."

Presentation: Have one or multiple members share their screen and give a short presentation, then open up to discussion.

Share a challenge: Each person has a chance to share a challenge that they want feedback on and then gets time for other participants to give them feedback.

Topic-based discussion: Have a topic or theme for the call, and leave it open to participants to jump in with their thoughts and opinions.

Commitment and next steps: Finish the discussion by asking each participant to share one commitment they will make as a result of the discussion, or a next action they will take.

I've found it's important to model the behavior you want your participants to bring to the discussion. If you want them to be vulnerable, then you should kick off with a vulnerable story. If you want them to ask a more technical question, give them an example with your own question.

I'd recommend keeping small-group discussions to 10 people or less and make sure to give people enough time. When someone invites me to a 30-minute discussion group with 15 people in it, you can count on me not coming. I know it's not going to work. Introductions take about 2 minutes per person. If you have a group of 15, you'll barely finish remembering everyone's favorite movie before the call is over. 90 minutes has become my sweet spot.

Tell Your Members How to Participate

Too often, we host an event, or post in an online community, and just hope that people will interact in a quality way without much guidance. There's a tendency a lot of community organizers have to be very hands off in their community spaces. They feel that it's important to give members the freedom to participate in the community however they want.

To some extent, this is true. You do want to give your members a fair amount of autonomy and creative freedom, because they'll come up with ways of interacting that you never would have thought of.

That said, the majority of members are looking for your guidance on how to contribute thoughtfully to the space. Ambiguity is stressful for someone who's new to an established community. All of those rituals and expressions of identity we spoke about earlier are new to them. They want someone to hold their hand through it. When someone shows up at an event, it can be incredibly intimidating. They don't know anyone yet, haven't gotten their lay of the land yet, and in a really big event there's an overwhelming amount of things to do.

Give them a map, tell them what to do first. Maybe you can connect every attendee with one other person when they enter to break the networking ice. If they arrive in time for breakfast, guide them to the breakfast table where they can ease into the event, grab a snack, and pick up casual conversations. If you want people in the audience to network with each other, give them questions to ask each other so they don't have to come up with topics themselves.

Onboarding is a great opportunity to be explicit in guiding members on how to participate in online spaces as well. When we welcome new members to the CMX online community, we don't just tell them to introduce themselves, we tell them how to introduce themselves and give them three specific questions to answer:

- Where are you from?
- What community are you building?
- What's one challenge that you're working through right now?

We'll mix up the questions sometimes and try different things, but we always give new members that guidance on how to participate.

Teach your members how to successfully ask the community for help. There's a tendency in online forums to ask very brief questions without a lot of guidance on how to answer the question. As a result, the member gets a whole range of different kinds of answers and all levels of quality.

For example, one of the most common questions in the CMX community is "What platform should we host our community on?" Without more guidance, there are a whole range of answers that people get that probably isn't exactly what the member was looking for. There's a good chance they'll get a lot of people answering and just saying, "We use X platform, it's great!" Not very helpful.

Instead, they could have provided more guidance to the rest of the community on how to participate in that thread. They could have said:

We're launching a new community and looking for a platform to host it on. I'd love to hear:

What platform you use.

What other platforms you considered.

Why you chose your current platform.

What do you like most about the platform?

What are your biggest issues with the platform?

Now I know how to answer their question more specifically. I don't have to guess what it is they were looking to learn. They were explicit about what quality participation looked like.

That's the power of communicating thoughtful guidelines on how to participate. Guidelines have the power to create an experience that's totally unique from anything else we experience in the world. They help us feel comfortable in an experience because we know how to participate in a valuable way. It's not left to us to figure it out. It teaches members how to work together more efficiently.

Before you invite your members into a space, whether it's a thread in a forum or an event you're organizing, be explicit about how you'd like people to participate in the space.

How to Get Members to Be Open and Vulnerable

Some of the most valuable community experiences a person will have is one where they have a chance to be truly open and vulnerable. We walk around most of our lives keeping things close to the chest. We often lack spaces where we can truly share how we're feeling, talk through personal challenges, and still feel supported and accepted. So when we finally do open up, it can be a true peak moment that we never forget, and we form a much deeper trust with the people we shared it with.

In the business world, we tend to avoid emotion as much as possible. "It's just business" rings true when you look at most community spaces hosted by organizations. Conversations are very product focused and surface level. But your customers, and everyone else in your community, is human. And there are absolutely challenges that are deep and personal that they're dealing with. Maybe they're struggling with something in their work or career and they haven't had a space to process it yet. You can create those spaces for them.

Intimacy is a requirement for opening up vulnerability amongst a group of people. It's very rare people will be truly open in a large group, or in a space that they aren't confident is private. To facilitate vulnerable interaction, you must have a small, private space.

Then, like we discussed in the previous section, you need to provide very specific rules and guidelines to make members confident that they're in a safe space.

One of my favorite examples of facilitating vulnerability is in the spaces hosted by the Inside Circle Foundation. A maximum security prison might be the last place you'd expect to find a group of men sitting in a circle, sharing their feelings, crying and supporting each other. But that's exactly what happens in these spaces.

The goal is to give the inmates a safe space to share openly in a way that they could not anywhere else in their lives. These men spend most of their life keeping their emotions to themselves. Weakness will result in a loss of status, or worse, loss of physical safety. Yet, they've all had serious trauma in their lives that they haven't been able to process. The Inside Circle Foundation gives them a safe space to process that trauma.

The results have been incredible. Members of the community have turned their lives around, gotten reduced sentences, and became volunteers in the program so they could help others.

How do you make men like this feel safe being open and vulnerable? Well, you need an incredible facilitator, first of all. When I spoke to Inside Circle Foundation's CEO James McLeary, I immediately felt a sense of trust and safety in his presence. He has a kind, yet strong demeanor, the kind of person you feel like you can share anything with and he'll listen without judgment.

When I asked him what the key has been for motivating the inmates participating in the program to be so open and vulnerable, he spoke about the rituals and rules that they put in place for every circle.

When every person enters the room, they stop, "take off their armor," and set it aside. The armor is imaginary of course, but the effect it has is very real. It lets everyone in that room know that they and every other person is there to be open, to be vulnerable, to share ...

Then, of course, there's what I like to call the "Vegas" rule: what's said here stays here. This is an extremely important rule, because the men will share things that could get them killed out in the yard. It's an important rule for any space where you want people to go deep. They want to know that only the people in the room will know about the things they share.

They start off every circle by reminding everyone of the rules and how to participate in the space. Those rules create the container for real deep conversations.

I got to experience this effect first hand in a workshop run by one of the best facilitators I've ever met, Ashanti Branch. Branch primarily works with young men of color to develop emotional maturity and live a life of intention. He leads a workshop called "Taking Off the Mask," which I had the opportunity to participate in. To kick things off, we all had a piece of paper where we drew our masks. We then had to write three words or phrases on the front that described the mask we show to the world, and three words on the back that described what we choose not to show the world.

We crumpled up our papers and had a "snowball fight," throwing the crumpled balls around the room, playing like kids.

After a few minutes, we were told to pick up a piece of paper and sit back down. Ashanti then asked for volunteers to stand up if something written on the paper they were holding resonated with them. We went around the room reading those messages out loud.

On the front, common words were "happy," "smart," "kind," "people pleaser." On the back, "fear," "stress," "death" ...

The energy in the room shifted, and suddenly felt heavy.

This is where Ashanti started setting the container for the next part of the experience.

He told us we're going to be sitting down in circles in groups of eight, and we'd go in order, each sharing our conclusion to the sentence, "You wouldn't know this by looking at me but ... "

He shared a few guiding statements: "Don't laugh. Don't respond. You can share anything you want, it doesn't have to be deep. It's okay to skip."

These rules were critical. They told us how to participate, what's okay or not okay. If someone made a joke, we knew we weren't supposed to laugh. We knew we weren't supposed to respond even when we feel compelled to comfort or add on. These rules resulted in an entirely unique experience from the norm.

The results were profound. It started off with people sharing fairly surface level things about themselves. "You wouldn't know this by looking at me, but I play basketball ... I cook ... I'm from Spain ... etc." But within a couple minutes, people started sharing some very personal things. "You wouldn't know this by looking at me, but I lost my father when I was five years old ... I have a lifelong illness ... I wake up hating myself every day ... "

I shared things with this group of strangers that I've never told anyone. We showed up in that space with an intention to learn more about ourselves, and be open with each other. The rules and guidelines provided by Branch gave us the roadmap for getting there.

Keep Your Rules Short and Simple to Start

Whether your goal is to drive vulnerability, or you just want to ensure that members have a quality experience in your community, you always want to have a clear policy with rules and guidelines for your community.

Keep your list of rules short and simple so that they're easy to remember. I recommend having no more than 10 rules and offer more detailed guidelines in your code of conduct. We have six rules in the CMX community. Start small and you'll likely add more organically over time as needed. Usually, you'll see something in your community that isn't very safe or high quality, realize you don't have a rule to account for it, and add it in.

Reddit had just three rules for the longest time, even as their community grew to millions of users. Only recently have they expanded their rules in order to fight growing toxicity on the platform. Now Reddit has eight rules:[3]

Rule 1

Remember the human. Reddit is a place for creating community and belonging, not for attacking marginalized or vulnerable groups of people. Everyone has a right to use Reddit free of harassment, bullying, and threats of violence. Communities and users that incite violence or that promote hate based on identity or vulnerability will be banned.

Rule 2

Abide by community rules. Post authentic content into communities where you have a personal interest, and do not cheat or engage in content manipulation (including spamming, vote manipulation, ban evasion, or subscriber fraud) or otherwise interfere with or disrupt Reddit communities.

Rule 3

Respect the privacy of others. Instigating harassment, for example by revealing someone's personal or confidential information, is not allowed. Never post or threaten to post intimate or sexually explicit media of someone without their consent.

Rule 4

Do not post or encourage the posting of sexual or suggestive content involving minors.

Rule 5

You don't have to use your real name to use Reddit, but don't impersonate an individual or an entity in a misleading or deceptive manner.

Rule 6

Ensure people have predictable experiences on Reddit by properly labeling content and communities, particularly content that is graphic, sexually explicit, or offensive.

Rule 7

Keep it legal, and avoid posting illegal content or soliciting or facilitating illegal or prohibited transactions.

Rule 8

Don't break the site or do anything that interferes with normal use of Reddit.

That's it. Pretty simple for the largest online community in the world.

Make your policy visible and easily accessible, and incorporate it into your onboarding experience. No one is going to read your terms of service unless they have a specific problem, so don't bury them in there. For live events, kick off by reviewing the rules and guidelines with your attendees. It shows your members that you're bringing intention to the event.

And whenever you share the rules, remind your members that they exist FOR them. The goal is to create a safe, high-quality experience for all of your members. Whenever I enforce a rule, I always close with "Thanks for helping us keep the community awesome," a reminder that the rules aren't personal, they're there for the community as a whole.

My Three Go-To Community Rules

There are a number of rules that I find myself using in most communities that I've launched or worked on. Three tend to show up the most:

1. What's Shared Here Stays Here

I mentioned this rule earlier and how it's used by the Inside Circle Foundation. I use this rule any time I have a small group discussion where I want people to be able to be open and honest with each other.

The Dinner Party, the potluck dinner community I wrote about in Chapter 2, is a great example of the power of this rule. They're a global community of people from their twenties to forties who have suffered the loss of a loved one. They come together in small groups, over potluck dinners, and engage in guided discussions.

Every person who comes to a dinner knows one of the core rules of the dinner, "What happens at the table, stays at the table." This simple phrase holds a lot of power. It's a key rule for creating safe spaces. Because when we share something, whether it's online or offline, we always take stock of who's in the room, who can hear us, and how they'll judge us based on what we say.

At a dinner table, you can assess that the people there will treat you with respect and hold space for you to share without judgment. But what about the people not at the table? What if someone at the table tells a friend what you said. You have no idea who that person is, and you know that since they're not participating in the same experience as you, that they aren't going to abide by the same rules and expectations as the group at the table. And so you share less than you would actually like to.

The "What's Shared Here Stays Here" rule solves for this problem. It's an agreement made by everyone present that nothing shared in the experience will be shared outside of their circle.

2. Give More Than You Take

There's no quicker way to let a community die than to just let everyone promote themselves and their products. A healthy community requires that members are contributing at least as much as they're taking out.

Self-promotion becomes a really big problem in communities where there's just one single feed of content, like in a Facebook Group. You won't have a dedicated space for people to share their own work, and your feed can quickly get overwhelmed with promotions.

If the value someone tries to get out of the community is just for themselves or their organization, their success isn't tied to the success of the community.

This is why I often implement "no self-promotion" where members cannot share links to their own content and products, outside of dedicated spaces specifically for that content. In our Facebook Group we do a "promo day" where members are free to promote their own links and articles. In Slack, we have a channel called #stuff-i-wrote.

People will argue that "my article is helpful to other community members!" That may be true, but people aren't great at judging the quality of their own work. Unless the community is curated so that you know everyone in there will be really thoughtful about what they share and why, it's better to have a blanket rule that sharing your own content and products isn't allowed.

This is the problem that has plagued LinkedIn groups for many years. Because everyone on LinkedIn is there for their own career advancement, they see groups as distribution channels for their content and products. They're not trying to contribute value to the community, they're trying to extract value. Most of those groups turn into what we call "link graveyards," a feed of people promoting their own stuff, and no one responding or engaging.

So just create a dedicated thread, or section, for promoting your own work, and don't allow it anywhere else in the community.

This is generally only a problem in online communities. The offline version is that person that goes to networking events and just hands out their business cards. It's clear they're not there to contribute, or develop relationships, they're just trying to extract value. They're not quality members of a community. If you're concerned this might happen in your event, then make a "no business card" rule, or require at least 10 minutes of conversation before a business card can be pulled out.

3. Critique the Idea, Not the Person

I'm a huge fan of facilitating healthy debate in community. I think we learn a lot more through thoughtful disagreement than we do through blind agreement.

That said, it's really important that you keep the criticism focused on the ideas, not on the person sharing the ideas.

We always have a rule that reminds people that we have a zero tolerance policy for hate speech and bullying. Focus on the ideas, don't attack the person.

A lot of communities keep this real informal at first. I've been a member of many communities who maintain just one rule, "Don't be an asshole." They usually update it to use a little less crass language over time, but the message remains the same. Treat each other with respect. Challenge ideas and aim to learn together. Don't put each other down.

Over time, you'll likely create a more comprehensive code of conduct around what exactly bullying and hate speech means, and what's allowed or not allowed in your community. While communities are small, these kinds of issues aren't usually as big of a concern. You can be more hands on at moderating. But once the community becomes really big, members will start testing the boundaries, and you'll need to get more specific.

Whatever your rules are, it's incredibly important that you make it clear to your community how those rules will be enforced, and that you do so consistently. If your members don't trust that rules will be enforced, then it's much more likely that they'll break the rules. Again, easier to manage when you're small. But when you have a large community, having clear standards become more important since you'll likely have a number of different moderators in the space, who all have to act consistently with each other. It's truly never too early to have a set of rules in place, and there are a lot of great templates available for free online today.

Using Metrics to Optimize Community Spaces and Experiences

When looking at measurement on the tactical level of your strategy, the goal is to identify metrics that will help you identify opportunities to improve your community spaces and experiences over time.

The three levels of your community strategy are all tied together. You create experiences and spaces, which will result in a more healthy and engaged community, which will drive business impact. This is how you can get a better grasp of how your day-to-day work building community is impacting the bottom line.

On the community and business levels of your community strategy, your measures are mostly looking backward, measuring the success and impact of the tactics and initiatives you worked on.

On the tactical level, measurement is all about action. It's predictive in that you should feel confident that the tactics you're working on will impact the health and engagement of your community. You're looking to get insights about what you can do to improve results in the future. It's all about asking the right questions, and using data and member feedback to get the answers.

For example, going back to Google's G2G program, a big question they wanted to answer is, "How can we improve instructor engagement?" They wanted more Googlers to volunteer to teach a class.

I recommended they look at a few different kinds of metrics and follow up with interviews:

- ◆ Look at the total number of classes taught per instructor. Interview instructors at different activity levels to find out what motivates their most active instructors.
- ◆ Survey instructors and ask them if they're getting value. Interview instructors who rate it highly and poorly to understand who the program is most and least valuable to, and why.
- ◆ Look at how many instructors taught one class then dropped. Interview them and find out how you can improve the instructor onboarding experience.

The insights from that data analysis and those interviews gave them a spread of specific tactics and initiatives they could focus on to address instructor objections and improve the instructor experience. They'd find ways to improve their instructor onboarding process and proactively address their biggest concerns and objectives. They'll get a better idea of what instructors' motivations are and can add in rewards and validation mechanisms to make sure they get that value. They'll also get a more clear idea of who an ideal candidate is to become an instructor so they can focus their outreach efforts.

By using the data to help them identify people to talk to, and using those conversations to identify tactics they can focus on for their community, they'll increase instructor engagement, improve the overall health and engagement of the community, and impact their organizational goals.

Another question we explored was, "How can we improve the quality of classes hosted by instructors?" All the classes are volunteer led, and the quality of those courses have a big impact on the overall experience in the community.

To answer that question, there were a few things they could do:

◆ Look at event ratings to identify which classes did well. Interview students who attended those classes to learn more about what they liked about their experience. They could then add those insights to the instructor guide.
◆ Look at total classes attended per student. Interview the most active and least active students to identify any themes in what made their classes so valuable, or what made them drop off.
◆ Sit in on classes and personally identify opportunities to improve.

This research provided the team with a range of specific tactics and initiatives they could focus on to improve the quality of classes and improve overall engagement in the community. They found that instructors weren't always clear on what makes a class great, and were able to provide them with more guidance and training. They got a better idea of who their ideal students were for the program, and focus their outreach on the right people. And they discovered some great ideas that they can make part of their standard format across all classes in the program. They'd then implement those changes and improvements, track the impact on overall community health and engagement, and measure the impact on their business outcomes.

You can take the same approach for any kind of community, online or offline, synchronous or asynchronous, to identify opportunities to improve engagement in your spaces and experiences.

Say you want to improve engagement in your online community. Use your analytics to tell you who your most active members are so you can interview them and get deeper insights into what motivates them to keep showing up.

You can identify the members who joined the community, took one action and never came back, and set up interviews with them, too. That'll give you great insights into how you can improve your onboarding process and engage your new members more effectively.

Running a support forum and want to increase the number of members who answer questions? Look at your member data to find your most active experts and survey them to find out more about their favorite and least favorite parts of the community. Identify people who have answered just three questions and see what you can learn about why they haven't answered more questions.

Whoever your contributors are in your community, and whatever kind of community you're organizing, you can take the same approach to figure out what you should be focusing on for the next month or quarter in order to improve engagement in your community and increase your impact on your business goals.

Notes

1. "The CMX Guide to Community Platforms, 2nd Edition [New . . . ." https:// cmxhub.com/cmx-guide-to-community-platforms/. Accessed 1 September 2020.
2. Dan Heath and Chip Heath, *The Power of Moments* (Random House UK, 2019).
3. "Content Policy – Reddit," Redditinc.com, 2019, https://www.redditinc .com/policies/content-policy. Accessed 23 August 2020.

Chapter 7

Activating Community Engagement

We've now gone through all three levels of your community strategy, and you have everything you need to develop a paint comprehensive plan!

But of course, a good plan will only take you so far. Even with the most perfect of plans, once you see it play out in reality, you might find that people are still reluctant to show up and participate. Motivating participation in your community is very much an art that takes iteration and tact.

So as we wrap up with this final chapter I'd like to share some of the key lessons I've learned in the community-building field about how to activate your community and move people to meaningfully engage in the spaces that you design and host.

I'll share the inside tips and tricks that have worked for me and the many community builders I've learned from.

Let's bring it home!

Engagement Is a Constant Experiment

My first big lesson is that engagement is all about trial and error. You need to try different things, and likely fail, to get to the approach that works for you and your community. All the success I've had in building community has come from constant experimentation.

You just don't know what people will organically want to engage with until you try it. You might have a great idea for a discussion prompt, but when you post, no one responds. Maybe the prompt wasn't worded perfectly, maybe it was a weird time of day where people weren't paying attention … who knows. And then sometimes you'll throw something out there for your community that you don't think is that interesting, and the community goes nuts with activity. The truth is, you just don't know, so you have to keep experimenting.

There's no step-by-step guide for building your specific community. The nuances of communities are what make each one so special. The little quirks that form, the common language members start using, the weird rituals … it all comes from someone doing something once, and it just sticks.

So don't be afraid of an event not working. Don't be afraid of a post getting no replies. In fact, you should expect things not to work a whole lot before it starts to work. And boom! When something works, keep doing it!

Keep innovating on how you bring your people together. Keep trying new things. Take risks. Be creative. People want to join a community that feels fresh and exciting. They don't want the same old experiences they can find anywhere else! Instead of hosting a standard webinar, open up a virtual speed-networking session. Instead of having a typical registration desk at your event, have volunteers welcome every attendee at the door and hand them the name of one other person they need to find at the event and say hello to.

Have fun! Get weird! You never know what will stick and become a new staple in your community.

Personal Invitations and "Doing Things That Don't Scale"

There's great power in a personal invitation.

When you personally invite someone to your community, it lets the person know that they were personally considered and approved. It makes them feel special and creates an understanding of intimacy and quality.

When first starting a community, personal invitations are the most powerful tool in your toolkit.

We avoid making personal invitations because it takes more time. It won't scale. But you're not focused on scale when launching a new forum or a new event, you're focused on building a strong foundation of quality and community. That's what a personal invitation does.

People have to respond to a personal invitation or risk looking like they're ignoring you. There's immediate social pressure in a personal invitation.

Instead of sending a mass email out to 1,000 customers asking them to join your new community, take the time to personally email 100 key people to jumpstart the community. Personalize each email a little bit. Each one will feel special for being personally invited and will be more likely to join and participate.

Instead of creating an RSVP page to your event and blasting it out to your email and social accounts, personally invite the right 20 people and just send the event details to them in an email. It lets them know that the event will be curated with good people and that they were personally selected.

You can use personal invitations to facilitate engagement as well. In the online communities I run, we always have a rule that every question must get at least three quality answers in 24 hours. If it's not happening organically, we make it happen. I'll start messaging other members privately and ask them to jump in and answer the question.

What most people do in this situation is post a comment to the whole community and ask, "Can anyone help answer this question?" It's too easy for everyone to ignore that ask. But if you personally message them and invite them to respond to the post, it will be much more obvious if they ignore it.

To the person who asked the question, it still looks like organic growth. They just see that a few people answered their question. To the person I ask to help, they feel good because I let them know that I consider them an expert and that they're helping the community in a meaningful way.

Whenever I take this approach, the answers to the question are always really thorough and thoughtful, because they feel like they're doing me a favor.

It's way too easy to ignore a public ask. It's nearly impossible to ignore a private, personal invitation. We also use this technique when welcoming members to the CMX community. We tag every new member who joins our community and ask them to introduce themselves. We do this because it makes them feel special, getting a personal tag, and because it makes them feel seen, which will increase the likelihood that they'll actually introduce themselves. If we just say, "Welcome everyone; please introduce yourselves!" it's too easy for them to fade into the crowd and choose not to participate.

People need to feel seen if they're going to participate. If they can just sit in the back row and blend in with the crowd, they mostly will. No one wants to be the first one to raise their hand.

If you've ever hosted an event or workshop, you know that the front row is always empty. Think back to the last time you were in a classroom or a workshop as a participant and the instructor asks for a volunteer to speak up. There's *always* an awkward silence as everyone looks around the room waiting for someone else to raise their hand. People just feel weird putting themselves in the front and raising their hand first.

I remember a long time ago, a speaker came to a startup accelerator I was participating in to teach the companies in our cohort about marketing. At the end of the class, he held out a $100 bill and said, "Who's going to step up and grab the opportunity?" encouraging us to get up and grab the bill from his hands. No one moved for a good 15 awkward seconds, until one person slowly got up and grabbed the bill from his hands and everyone laughed. Everyone was so afraid to be the first mover, even if there was a $100 reward in it. The speaker was making a point about how we often see opportunities to strike, but we hesitate because we're afraid to be the first mover, afraid of being wrong or getting embarrassed.

It's the same in communities. You'll find that people will wait for someone else to post the first comment before jumping into a thread. Or they'll wait for someone else to speak up in a group discussion before they say anything. It's in part because they want to create space for others to speak. It's in part because they're afraid of being embarrassed or putting themselves out there. As community builders, we often avoid doing things like writing personal invitations because it takes a long time and a lot of work but that's exactly what it takes to get a community off the ground. Remember, Sarah Leary, the Cofounder of Nextdoor, went door to door asking neighbors to join the platform. Pretty hard to ignore that invitation!

Remember, a community organically taking off from day one is the exception, not the rule. The community builders that succeed at getting a community off the ground are hustling behind the scenes to ensure that engagement is happening.

Every member who enters the community feels personally welcomed. Every person who shows up at the event has someone meaningful to talk to. Every person who posts in your community gets quality responses. You need to be "behind the curtain" making introductions, facilitating discussions, and putting in the work to get the wheels of community turning.

Over time, your community will develop organic engagement. Referring back to the community lifecycle, in the growth stage you'll start to see more organic engagement in the community, and by the time it gets to maturity, most engagement will be organic.

But even then, you'll likely be launching new spaces, organizing new events, and working to motivate members to participate in new and unique ways.

Don't wait for them to engage. Make it happen.

Ask for Permission

A big part of making people feel like they're a part of a community is ensuring that they feel like they have influence over what happens. In the sense of community theory, which we covered in Chapter 1, the exchange of influence is an important element in someone feeling like they belong to the group. The community has influence over the members, but the individual members also need to feel like they have influence over the community.

Member influence shows up in all sorts of big and small ways in a community. The language you as the community organizer use, and the way you facilitate, can impact that experience.

A key way you can consistently make your members feel more influential is to always ask for permission when you'd like to do something. It's a subtle but powerful difference in facilitating engagement.

For example, say you're hosting a conference and you want everyone in the audience to turn to each other and introduce themselves. You have two ways you can go about facilitating that experience.

The first way, which is what most people do, is to just tell them to do it. "OK, we're going to do some quick networking with your neighbors! Please turn to the person next to you and tell them one fun fact about yourself!"

People will do it, and networking will ensue. But the second way you could facilitate that experience is to ask for permission. "I'd love to create more opportunities for all of you to get to meet some new people at this event, and so I'd love to facilitate a quick networking experience for you and your neighbors. Are you interested in doing that?"

The audience would let out a chorus of "Yes! Sure! I guess so! etc.," and then you can move into the experience.

The general outcome is the same; people will do what you wanted them to do and they will network. But there's something powerful about inviting people to participate in an experience and letting them opt in instead of telling them to participate in an experience that will help you get more buy-in.

Let's say you want members in a group discussion to be more open and vulnerable. You could say, "This is a safe space, so feel free to share openly!" Or you could ask for permission and say, "I know this conversation will be more valuable for everyone if we can all be more open and vulnerable with each other. Would you all like to make a commitment to sharing really honestly and transparently in this space?"

Asking instead of telling gives the members control over the experience, and makes it more likely that they'll lean into the experience.

Don't Fear the Crickets

No matter how much you work to make people feel seen, use personal invitations, and politely voluntell people to participate, there will still be times when you just don't get a response to something you organize for the community.

I don't know about you, but when I was younger, one of the worst fears in the world was that no one would show up to my birthday party. I would feel a terrible dread that no one would show up and I'll be horribly embarrassed.

It's a feeling we're all too familiar with today, thanks to social media. We're constantly putting ourselves out there, sharing stories, telling jokes, giving our hot takes, and just hoping that people like what we have to say. I'm certainly guilty of deleting a tweet after not getting enough likes in the first 15 minutes.

For community builders, this fear tends to show up constantly because it's literally our job to get people to engage in our spaces. We worry that we'll organize a meetup and no one will show up, that we'll post a discussion in our online community, that we'll put ourselves out there and just get … crickets …

If you're going to be successful at building community, you have to get over this fear. You have to get comfortable with the idea that some of what you post will not get a lot of engagement, especially in the early days of building community. Because I guarantee you, it will happen. You will try something new and it won't click with the community. You will get awkward silences and low response rates.

The good news is that if you post in an online community and no one responds, there's a good chance they didn't even see it. So there's nothing to be embarrassed about! And if they did, they just kept scrolling and didn't give it a second thought. That's the beauty of online communities. People only really see the content that works. The content that doesn't work gets buried pretty quick.

If you host an event and only a few people show up, flip it around and make it an "intimate experience." I've had a stage and seating set up for a big event that only 10 people showed up to before and decided to just ditch the stage, put the chairs in a circle, and bring the speaker in for an intimate discussion. That gave us the opportunity to go much deeper with the people in the room, which we wouldn't have been able to have with 50 people. Was it a little embarrassing? Sure! But you can't let that stop you from taking risks and trying new things in your community.

And more good news – over time, the odds of crickets will get lower and lower. You'll grow your community, develop your reputation, and there will be more people who are already active in your space, more likely to be there to engage with your content.

Getting good at anything requires going through a lot of failure. Want to raise money? You'll hear no from a lot of investors. Want to record a hit song? You'll probably write a lot of really bad songs first. And if you want to build a community, and create engaging content for your community, you'll need to create a lot of content and host a lot of events that just won't work. It's an art, and art takes risk.

Keep at it. Host another event and work harder to promote it. Post again tomorrow and try something different. Or just delete it and post something else; I won't tell anyone. Just don't let the crickets get you down. Keep showing up and creating consistently in your community, no matter what.

Talk Funny

It doesn't matter if your community is professional, or focused on a serious topic; humor is pretty much always welcome. It gives people a momentary feeling of joy, that hit of dopamine and a natural spike to the most boring of content. It can break up awkward silences and tensions, loosens people up and make them feel more relaxed in your space. It can make a boring topic exciting. Humor will almost always make your content better.

You might think you're not a funny person, but according to my very Irish friend David Nihill, who wrote the bestselling book *Do You Talk Funny?*, anyone can learn to be funny. He was deathly afraid of public speaking and decided the best way to overcome that fear was to commit to standup comedy. Not a very wise choice, but one he made Guinness free.

Over the course of his journey, he founded a community and conference around making boring content fun(ny), filmed a comedy special, and won the prestigious San Francisco International Comedy Competition – a month-long test of your funny endurance whose previous finalists include Robin Williams, Ellen DeGeneres, and Dana Carvey. Along the way, he picked up on tools anyone can use to, well, be funnier (if being Irish alone didn't count). Here's what he taught me.

Find the Funny in Failure, Frustration, and Pain Points

"To truly laugh, you must be able to take your pain and play with it," Charlie Chaplin said. While he likely didn't mean community pain points, the same wisdom applies. Start by looking at your fails and your firsts. The first time you did something wrong. People love the humility and openness, and if something is embarrassing for you, it's likely funny for me. Also, the safest humor involves personal stories because they are guaranteed to be original and can be easily practiced and perfected. Plus, if nobody laughs, worst case you just told them a story. Jokes have a high chance of failure. Stories do not.

Use the Rule of Three

"This rule is a basic structure for jokes and ideas that capitalize on the way we process information," says Nihill. "We have become proficient at pattern recognition by necessity. Three is the smallest number of elements required to create a pattern. This combination of pattern and brevity results in memorable content. Create a pattern with the first two elements and break it with the third."

For example, Jon Stewart once joked, "I celebrated Thanksgiving in an old-fashioned way. I invited everyone in my neighborhood to my house, we had an enormous feast, and then I killed them and took their land."

Pointed as always, Jon.

Put the Word the Humor Hinges on at the End of the Sentence

Humor is all about the delivery. In general, you want to put the key word in your joke at the end of your statement. For example, if you tell a joke about a cat and the fact it's a cat is the surprise or twist, don't say, "There was a cat in the box." Say, "In that box was a cat." That way you facilitate a reaction.

Crowdsource Your Comedy

Imagine you had a whole community of people you could reach out to and ask to share their experiences, frustrations, and funny happenings on any given topic! Wait. You're a community builder. You do!

Ask your community members for their funny and embarrassing stories. It'll make for a lively discussion, and you'll get a ton of content to use in future posts.

Call Out Awkward Silences

Humor can take the air out of awkwardness when no one responds to your post or raises their hand. One of my favorite things to do when no one responds to my post in a community is comment again and say, "Bueller...? Bueller...?" or, "Guess everyone's sleeping in this Monday, huh?" or, "I thought I was good at this whole community engagement thing!" with a little winky emoji to really communicate how funny I think I'm being. I didn't say I'm funny to everyone.

Nihill explains how comedians use this same technique when a joke flops. To take the tension out of the air, they'll make a comment like, "Well, my mom thought that was funny."

Audiences hate awkward silences as much as you do. Humor gives you all an escape.

How to Spark Great Debates

I've mentioned in this book already that I'm a big fan of facilitating healthy, respectful debates in communities. Thoughtful disagreement helps us learn a lot more about a topic than groupthink and blind agreement. It forces us to consider new perspectives and understand a topic from different angles.

When I was in Model Congress in high school, I enjoyed having to argue the side that I personally disagreed with, because it forced me to see the other side and really think through the holes in my argument. As long as it doesn't get personal, debates are a really effective exercise for collective learning.

I also think that healthy disagreement will make a community stronger. When a group of people can enter into a disagreement and treat each other with respect and kindness, they come out the other side of that experience with more trust and will feel more connected.

In Chapter 6, I shared one of my favorite rules, "Critique the idea, not the person." This rule is critical for facilitating respectful disagreements, and I always remind members to keep this rule in mind when I kick off a new debate.

You can facilitate debates in a number of ways.

First off, when kicking off a debate in an online community, I always make it clear that I'm intending to start a debate. This helps members understand that we're engaging in a thought exercise to learn together, rather than a personal, emotional disagreement. I'll start off and say something like, "There's been a lot of discussion on this topic, and I'd love to kick off a proper debate so we can

David Spinks
☉ Admin · December 12, 2017 · **☉**   •••
Debate:
We shouldn't separate community management from social media management. They can both be part of the "community department".

FIGURE **7.1**

explore both arguments." Or in spaces where the community is already familiar with the format because I've done it before, I'll just say, "Debate: … " and kick it off with a prompt for discussion.

Figure 7.1 shows an actual post from our community that sparked a great discussion.

Another way to make a debate more engaging and effective is to make your prompt a statement that they need to agree or disagree with, rather than leaving it open-ended.

Say you're organizing a community for runners and wanted to start a debate about barefoot running and whether it's actually good for you. What people often do is post and say, "Do you think barefoot running is good for you?" Simple enough, and you'll likely get some members responding with their thoughts.

But a more effective way to prompt a debate and motivate people to respond would be to phrase it as "Debate: Barefoot running is better for you than using running shoes. Agree or disagree?"

This immediately makes the member wonder to themselves which side they sit on. And they'll be more likely to participate because, well, people like to make their opinions known and tend to enjoy a good, friendly debate with two sides.

When I share this advice, some people express concern that it's too divisive and can cause unnecessary conflict in your community. Andrea Middleton, the Open Source Community Growth Strategist at Automatic is an expert in conflict management. In her over ten years of experience, she's learned that, "Our jobs as leaders is not to remove all conflict. Conflict is a valuable tool that can benefit the community. Diverse communities have conflict because you're bringing different thoughts together into a synthesized whole. So it's not about getting rid of conflict, but preventing it from escalating to a point where it breaks the relationships that we need to collaborate."

Middleton breaks down community conflict into five levels:

1. Difference – members have a different preference or taste that they are both comfortable with
2. Misunderstanding – a member doesn't have the same information as another member and think they disagree but they just don't have the full story
3. Disagreement – members actually disagree and feels discomfort about the disagreement, creating strain on the relationship
4. Discord – one party identifies a trend of disagreements over time creating significant strain on the relationship
5. Polarization – the relationship is actively hostile and members may refuse to engage in constructive behaviors.

"You want to keep all conflicts in level 1 and 2", says Middleton. "You can edge into level 3, but you don't want to stay there for long."

Conflict is going to happen in your community whether you facilitate it or not. It's natural for humans to disagree, take sides, and want to make their point. So I'd argue that it's better to teach them how to debate respectfully in your community so that when a controversial topic does come up, they've built up that muscle already.

And I believe that conflict in a community can be a good thing. It's how that conflict is processed and how people treat each other during the conflict that matters. If they attack the person and not the idea, that's a recipe for toxicity. If they can keep the conversation focused on the ideas, and on learning from each other's perspectives, it will actually deepen the sense of connection and belonging within the group.

Debates are a really useful framework for going deeper into a topic than you normally would. It forces your members to consider different perspectives and really think through their arguments. As a result, everyone learns more.

Moderation Is Never Personal

Anyone who decides to bring people together will inevitably find themselves in the position of having to moderate their members.

This is an uncomfortable position for a lot of community professionals since you're also developing personal relationships with members, and even friendships. If you're as conflict-averse as I am, there's nothing worse than having to moderate a member of the community that you care about, and have them get really upset with you.

A technique I use here is to remove the personal aspect of rule enforcement. I do this in a few ways.

First, like we discussed in Chapter 6, have a clear set of rules that members agree to when they join. This "agreement" is something you can then call back to. "As you know, everyone in the community has agreed to these rules." Now it's not about your opinion – you have no opinion in the situation, it's just the rule that the community has agreed to. If we want to revisit the rules, we can totally do that, but for the moment, these are the rules.

Second, I always make it about benefiting the community, not about anything that I want. I would never say, "I want you to follow the rules" or "I prefer that you don't do that … " I'll say, "these rules exist in order to make this community great for everyone," and I'll always close with something like "Thanks for helping us keep this community awesome." It's not about me, it's about the whole.

You can still be empathetic. "I know this is unusual in online communities," or, "I know you didn't intend to break the rule." That empathy will increase the warmth of your otherwise impersonal message.

There comes a point where it's impossible for it to not get personal. Maybe a member is attacking you personally or showing up in other spaces online to continue to let you know how upset they are.

If things ever get out of hand, I always recommend getting on the phone with the person and talking one-to-one. It's so much harder to navigate highly emotional issues in a text-only online space. Too much gets lost in translation. And if it's a public space, there will always be a performative element to the interaction, since you both know that others are watching. Getting on a call will allow you to talk human-to-human, and make sure they feel heard.

I always go into any conversation with someone I'm "moderating" assuming good intentions. I always give them the benefit of the doubt. But I make sure that they're aware of the impact they're having on other members. Maybe they were unaware of the rules. Maybe they didn't quite see how their tone was coming across. Sometimes, they just don't think that anyone is listening and don't feel accountable (especially in anonymous or pseudonymous communities) and hearing from an actual person will catch them completely off guard, making them feel accountable once again.

You never know what kind of day someone is having, and what they're dealing with in their personal life that might have brought them to bring negativity into your space. Lead with empathy. Actively listen. It's not uncommon for your biggest detractors to become your biggest advocates if you put in the work to really make them feel heard.

Sometimes, no matter how well you communicate, a member will continue to attack and harass you or other members of the community, or continue to break the rules. If this happens, then you need to have a policy in place for suspending and banning members that you can enforce. Make that policy clear for all members up front so there's no confusion around what happens when rules are violated. Don't take on more toxicity from members than you have to before making the decision to remove a member. As the community leader, you need to take care of yourself and your members first.

Default to Transparency and Admit Your Mistakes

Failure to be transparent has driven many communities into the pit of misery.

Digg is one of the most famous examples. Once a thriving community for sharing content on the web, the downward spiral began when sweeping changes were made to the platform without being properly communicated to the members of the platform, who left en masse (leading to the rapid rise of Reddit).

Trust is like a cup of water that you fill up slowly over time by being consistently honest and doing right by people. When you mess up and people feel like you wronged them, the cup gets emptied. But you can actually fill it back up more full than it was before by owning and responding to the mistake in the right way.

You have to fully own your mistakes, apologize sincerely, and involve the community in taking clear and decisive action to remedy the issue.

I always default to transparency whenever faced with a decision or a challenge in the community. If there's a situation that I don't know how to navigate, I'll share that challenge with the community up front and ask for their feedback.

For example, when we were considering whether CMX should be acquired by Bevy, my biggest concern was the objectivity of the community, and the trust that we had with our members. I didn't want our members to feel like CMX was now biased since it was owned by another company that has a product to sell. So I just brought that concern to the community and shared openly what I was worried about. I posted threads in our public community and set up calls with some of our longest-standing members.

That vulnerability led to a really thoughtful, open discussion that the entire community could engage in around a topic that was really important to all of us. It turned out that members weren't really concerned about us losing objectivity because they trusted us. And they were mostly just really happy that the community and the team would get a lot more resources and support to be able to do the work.

It's not always so positive. We once had a group of members, when we've made a mistake, we acknowledge that mistake publicly in the community, own it, apologize, and share the steps we're taking to fix the mistake.

When in doubt, I always default to transparency. When our community sends us private feedback on what they want to see improved at CMX Summit, we summarize their feedback and share it back out (anonymized) so that everyone can see what the feedback was.

When you don't know how to handle a situation in the community, tell your members that. When you have a big decision to make, share that decision with your community.

By trusting your community, you're teaching them to trust you, too.

Use Your Authentic Voice

A big difference between marketing and community is that when you post a message from a brand, you generally want to use a consistent "brand voice." But when you're facilitating a community, you're usually doing so as an individual, using your own personal identity.

For businesses that are new to community, they'll often try to maintain that same brand voice in their community. But it's really important that you, as the community leader, use your own personal voice.

When you adapt your voice to sound like a brand, but you're using your personal name and identity, it comes across as robotic and insincere. People don't want to engage with a brand, they want to engage with a person.

Of course, you don't want your community team to adopt a voice that's in direct conflict with your brand voice. It's something to consider when hiring someone whose job it is to engage in the community. Is their authentic voice aligned with your values and culture? If not, they may not be the right fit for your community.

Now, like a great writer, a lot of community professionals can adapt and bring a voice to the community that they believe is right for that group of people. We all adapt our voice based on who's in the room. I speak with my closest friends differently than I speak to people at temple or at a networking event. But whenever I engage in a community, I always try to bring my authentic, personal voice.

My personal voice is more casual and conversational. Perhaps you've picked up on that in this book. It's the same voice I bring any time I post in a community I'm managing. I don't try to adapt to a brand voice. I want members to feel like they're hearing from a human; from me. I try to keep the content relatable, like they're talking to a friend.

You may have to remind your community team of this. I've hired community managers before who felt hesitant to post in the community because they were trying to replicate my voice, thinking that we all needed to have the same voice. I always encourage them to use their own voice. By using their own voice, they'll be able to connect with people who don't feel as connected to me and my voice. Having a diverse community team with unique voices will help you connect with more people in the community.

Arlan Hamilton, the founder of Backstage Capital, has overcome extreme challenges, going from being homeless and living in her car to successfully launching a venture capital fund focused on investing in underestimated founders. Within a minute of talking to Arlan or reading her content, you know you're hearing her authentic voice, because she sounds nothing like the majority of venture capitalists out there. She's as real as it gets. A while back I asked her for her advice to other community leaders. She said, "Always be yourself, so that the people looking for you can find you." It's stuck with me ever since. Using your real voice will make it possible for people who are looking for your message, and your tone, to feel connected to you and to the community. Your voice just might be how someone else finds belonging.

When posting in an online community, speaking at an event, or interacting with people in most any way, just be yourself. Don't try to be a brand. Don't try to be a "leader," whatever that means. Just be a person who's there to serve the community, and hopefully give your members a lot of value.

Of course, this doesn't mean there shouldn't be guide rails. Every company should have a voice and tone that will guide employees in how to respond thoughtfully, nonviolently, and effectively in different situations. But within those guide rails, insert yourself. Bring your own flavor.

The subtle personalization can make all the difference in the world. Maybe it's a "y'all" or the overuse of ellipses as I tend to do … whatever is true to you.

People can pick up on it, even (especially?) in text.

If you feel like you don't know how to translate your personal voice to your writing, then record yourself speaking the post, and then write down what you said. If you can write like you speak, it will come across more natural, and your members will feel more connected to you.

Keep Your Energy High and Positive

I'm a big believer in radical positivity for anyone who's building communities.

If you've ever been a part of a community that was really pessimistic, you know how it feels. It breeds toxicity, anger, and the wrong kind of conflict.

It starts with leadership and the example that you set for your community. Positivity is contagious. Your energy, whatever it is, is contagious. How you act in your community will be how your community members act.

If you show up and bring a lot of positivity in your space every day, that will set the tone and the example for other members to follow. If you're super negative, that gives members permission to be negative, too.

Culture always starts at the top. How you act sets the standard for what's OK in the community.

◆ If you're negative, they'll be negative.
◆ If you're witty, they'll be witty.
◆ If you post cat gifs, they'll post cat gifs.
◆ If you promote your own content, they'll promote their own content.
◆ If you try to show up with positive energy every day, they'll try to do the same.
◆ If you're transparent and vulnerable, they'll be transparent and vulnerable.

Humans try to find the norm when they enter a new space. What are people doing? How are they acting? What's the energy like? We read the room and adjust how we act based on what we see. *Energy* might sound hippy dippy, but it's real, and it's up to you to bring the right kind of energy to the room. People can feel it. We run through this kind of analysis every time we arrive in a social space, online or offline.

Different communities may thrive on different kinds of energies. You have to know your audience. You don't want to show up grinning ear to ear and acting all chipper in a community about death. You don't want to throw out cuss words in a professional community unless you're intentionally going for that kind of tone like the Fuck Cancer movement, who says right up front, "We are sorry if you are offended or have a problem with the word FUCK; we are offended and have a problem with the word CANCER."

So when I say high energy, I don't mean you have to be bouncing off the walls, and when I say positive, I don't mean you have to vibe like a yoga teacher. By high energy, I mean you should come with a genuine enthusiasm for your work and for your community. By positive, I mean avoid being overly pessimistic. You can be critical and realistic, without being a downer. Positivity doesn't mean there isn't disagreement or conflict. But you can still go into a disagreement with a positive mindset, and a focus on learning and understanding each other.

Now, remember that you have leaders in your community who can also swing the energy of your community. If someone gets upset with your organization about something, and vocalizes it, they can rally other members and change the energy in your community in an instant.

You can't control the tone that your members want to take. And it's very easy to misinterpret tone in online spaces where everyone is using text. It can be beneficial to bolster your content with emojis, emoticons, or even gifs/images to make your tone more clear. But when reviewing members' posts, it can be hard to tell. Are they typing in all caps because they're angry or excited? Or maybe they're just being sarcastic, the hardest tone to identify online.

Even if you feel confident that someone is coming in with a lot of negativity, you shouldn't "tone police" them. That will just make them more upset and potentially cover up an important point they're trying to make.

This is a common challenge for people of color who rightfully express anger with unjust experiences, just to be told that they should take a better tone if they want people to listen to them. Instead of trying to control anyone's tone, just meet them with positivity and understanding. You can control your own tone, and there's a good chance that your positivity and calm will help others find their calm too.

This also works well for trolls. My favorite way to respond to trolls is to "kill them with kindness." They'll say something really rude, probably looking for an in-kind reaction, and I'll respond with something like, "It sounds like you're having a really rough day today. Sending you lots of good positive vibes!" They'll either disappear, tell me to go f*** myself, or on rare occasions, respond with something like, "Wow! I was not expecting that response, I appreciate that. I am having a rough time … "

By creating an ongoing standard of positivity and support in your community, you can lessen the intensity of the ebbs and flows in your community. If someone wants to be really negative, but they're bringing that energy into a sea of positivity, it will be harder for that negativity to spread.

Use exclamation points liberally in your online communities! Bring the joy! You want your community to be a space where people can find positivity and joy, especially if they're struggling with something in their lives that's bringing them a lot of negativity outside of your community.

On the hard days, the days where you don't feel like building the community anymore, the days where you're frustrated with your members, the days where your personal life is weighing on you, just remember that how you act in your community, as the leader, will be the example that your members follow. If you need to step away and come back when you're in a better place, then step away.

That's why self-care is so important for community builders. You need to take care of yourself in order to take care of others. If your cup is empty, and you're giving energy you don't have to your community, you will burn out. Take care of yourself and recharge so that you can bring your best self to your community, and set a positive example.

Sometimes negativity becomes a big issue for companies when it's being directed at their products. For companies that are worried about opening up a forum because they're afraid of customers complaining about their product and being really negative, your fear is not unfounded.

But my question for you is, would you rather have people speaking negatively in a space where you have visibility and influence, or would you rather them talk about your product negatively in a place where you have no visibility or control?

The reality is, if they don't like something about your product, they're going to be negative about it somewhere. By hosting that space, you actually have an opportunity to show up, listen, make them feel heard, and bring radical positivity into every action.

You'll find that a lot of customers will change their tune when they feel like a real person is listening to them, acknowledging their concerns, discussing solutions, and doing it all with a big, authentic smile on their face.

Go Forth and Build Community!

As we arrive at the end of our journey, I hope you feel fully equipped to go forth and build thriving communities for your business!

Here's a cheat sheet you can use to remember some of the big frameworks we discussed throughout the book:

Strategy Level	Focus	Frameworks
Business	The business outcomes your community program will drive for your company.	The SPACES Model (Chapter 2)
Community	How your community will grow and become more healthy and engaged over time.	The Social Identity Cycle (Chapters 3–5)
Tactical	The specific initiatives and improvements you work on in order to build a healthy, engaged community and achieve the business outcomes.	The 7Ps of Community Experience Design (Chapter 6)

I hope I've fulfilled my promise to you, and you're finishing this book feeling more confident and prepared to successfully build meaningful communities that will have incredible impact on your business and everyone it touches.

Your learning journey doesn't stop here! I encourage you to keep learning everything you can about building community. And I invite you to join our community at CMX (http://cmxhub.com) to grow alongside thousands of other community builders, founders, and professionals, and go deeper with our training and research.

I believe that community is truly the future of business. There's just too much opportunity and value to ignore. Community-driven businesses will grow faster and have a bigger positive impact on the world by always leading with a "Community First" value.

Profit at the expense of people is no way to build a sustainable, long-lasting business, and it will take more away from society than it puts in. When you make any decision for your company, always look at it through the lens of the question, "How does this serve our community?" Let that question be your North Star to ensure that you're focusing on initiatives that are good both for people and for your bottom line.

It's not an either/or situation. Companies can build real communities and rapidly grow their revenue and value. There are some occasions where you may find yourself leaning more on the revenue side and losing sight of the community. Notice when that's happening and make it a priority to refocus on the people your company impacts. Figure out how you can build community and grow your business, without sacrificing one for the other.

Community building is among the most important work in the world. You're giving people a sense of belonging and a space to safely express their authentic identities. There will never be a time that humans don't need community, and in modern society, there's a good chance we'll only need it more in years to come.

Now go forth and build the communities the world needs most!

Bibliography

Ariely, Dan. *Predictably Irrational: The Hidden Forces That Shape Our Decisions*. New York: Harper Perennial, 2010.

"Content Policy – Reddit." Redditinc.com, 2019. www.redditinc.com/policies/content-policy.

CMX, The 2020 *Community Industry Trends Report*. CMX, 2019. cmxhub.com/community-industry-trends-report-2020.

Deci, Edward L., Richard Koestner, and Richard M. Ryan. "A Meta-Analytic Review of Experiments Examining the Effects of Extrinsic Rewards on Intrinsic Motivation." *Psychological Bulletin* 125, no. 6 (1999): 627–668. doi.org/10.1037/0033-2909 .125.6.627.

Duhigg, Charles. *Power of Habit : Why We Do What We Do in Life and Business*. New York: Random House Trade Paperbacks, 2014.

"First Round State of Startups 2019." stateofstartups2019.firstround.com, 2019. stateofstartups2019.firstround.com/.

Heath, Dan, and Chip Heath. *The Power of Moments*. Random House UK, 2019.

Hsieh, Tony. "How I Did It: Zappos's CEO on Going to Extremes for Customers." *Harvard Business Review* (July 1, 2010). hbr.org/2010/07/how-i-did-it-zappos-ceo-on-going-to-extremes-for-customers.

Iriberri, Alicia, and Gondy Leroy. "A Life-Cycle Perspective on Online Community Success." *ACM Computing Surveys* 41, no. 2 (February 1, 2009): 1–29. doi.org/ 10.1145/1459352.1459356.

Kendi, Ibram X. *How to Be an Antiracist*. One World; First Edition (August 13, 2019) (Vintage, 2020.

Kim, Amy Jo. "Introduction to Game Thinking." *Medium* (June 8, 2018). medium .com/@amyjokim/introduction-to-game-thinking-6e7273e68cc9.

McMillan, David W., and David M. Chavis. "Sense of Community: A Definition and Theory." *Journal of Community Psychology* 14, no. 1 (January 1986): 6–23. doi .org/10.1002/1520-6629 (198601)14:1<6::aid-jcop2290140103>3.0.co;2-i.

Mohr, Tara Sophia. "Why Women Don't Apply for Jobs Unless They're 100% Qualified." *Harvard Business Review* (March 2, 2018). hbr.org/2014/08/why-women-dont-apply-for-jobs-unless-theyre-100-qualified.

Nelson, Suzi. "How DigitalMarketer Activated 44% of Silent Community Members | Case Study." DigitalMarketer (March 18, 2020). www.digitalmarketer.com/blog/ activate-community-members/.

Nir Eyal. *Hooked : How to Build Habit-Forming Products. Norwick*: Penguin Books, 2016.

Pepitone, Albert, and Leon Festinger. "A Theory of Cognitive Dissonance." *The American Journal of Psychology* 72, no. 1 (March 1959): 153. doi.org/10.2307/1420234.

Ryan, Richard M., and Edward L. Deci. "Self-Determination Theory and the Facilitation of Intrinsic Motivation, Social Development, and Well-Being." *American Psychologist* 55, no. 1 (2000): 68–78. doi.org/10.1037/0003-066x.55.1.68.

Tajfel, H. "Social Identity and Intergroup Behaviour." *Social Science Information* 13, no. 2 (April 1, 1974): 65–93. doi.org/10.1177/053901847401300204.

"TechSmith Saves $500,000 by Crowdsourcing Snagit on Mac Development Research in Custom Get Satisfaction Community." *Business Wire* (April 19, 2011). www.businesswire.com/news/home/20110419005155/en/TechSmith-Saves-500000-Crowdsourcing-Snagit-Mac-Development.

About the Author

David Spinks launched his first online community at 14 years old for his favorite video game, *Tony Hawk's Pro Skater 4*. He's now a prominent leader in the community-driven business movement and has trained and advised community teams at companies like Google, Facebook, Udemy, Waze, and Airbnb. Spinks has long believed that community is the future of business and has made it his life's purpose to help others learn how to build thriving, meaningful communities. He is the founder of CMX, where over 20,000 community professionals gather to learn and support each other, and is the host of CMX Summit, the largest conference in the community industry. In 2019, CMX was acquired by Bevy, where Spinks now serves as the VP of Community, helping companies launch and scale event-driven community programs. Spinks grew up in New York, currently lives in San Francisco with his wife and son, and can usually be found hiking or playing basketball in his free time (when he's not injured). You can follow and message him on twitter @davidspinks, where he regularly shares his observations and lessons on community.

Acknowledgments

This book would not exist without the passion, generosity, and energy of every CMX team member, community leader, speaker, and member over the years.

Big thank you to Max Altschuler, who helped me make CMX a reality when it was just a dream and to Carrie Melissa Jones, who worked with me to take the CMX community to incredible heights over the community's first few years.

Thank you to Steven Broudy, Carrie Melissa Jones, Evan Hamilton, and Erica McGillivray for their feedback and contributions on CMX models and frameworks shared in this book.

Thank you to Evan Hamilton, Erica McGillivray, and Ann-Marie Pawlicki, who each helped make CMX Summit into an industry-shaping event during their time running the show. Thank you to Beth McIntyre, Katie McCauley, Samuel Weber, and Yrja Oftedahl for helping make the CMX community into the special place it is today.

Thank you to Derek Andersen for believing in the vision of CMX and helping the community reach all new heights, and to everyone on the Bevy team for their hard work on and advocacy for the CMX community.

Thank you to Danya Shults, Caty Kobe, Camille Ricketts, Carrie Melissa Jones, Reina Pomeroy, Evan Hamilton, Tim Parkin, Rob Hanna, and James Augeri for their edits and feedback on this book.

Thank you to my wife, Alison Malfesi, for supporting me through the many long days and late nights it took to make this book a reality.

Thank you to my son, Lucca, for waiting to be born until the week after I turned in my manuscript.

Thank you to my parents, Ian and Revital Spinks, for always believing in me, and teaching me how to lead with kindness, ambition, and empathy.

Thank you to my coach, Jennifer Akullian, for helping me stay sane throughout the book-writing process, to Hiten Shah for mentoring me through the highs and lows of building CMX, and to Jonathan Howard for being in my corner every step of the way.

Thank you to my editor, Mike Campbell, and my agent, Sarah Fuentes, for believing in this book and helping me make it as good as it could be.

Thank you to all of our CMX hosts who work so hard to bring together the community professionals in their local cities around the world. Thank you to every CMX member who has contributed to the community and shown up for another member when they needed it.

And thank you to every person out there who's working to build community. You're doing some of the most important work in the world. Please keep building.

Index